Thomas Sinclair

Caithness Events
A Discussion of Captain Kennedy's Historical Narrative, and ....

ISBN/EAN: 9783337234393

Printed in Europe, USA, Canada, Australia, Japan

Cover: Foto ©ninafisch / pixelio.de

More available books at **www.hansebooks.com**

Thomas Sinclair

Caithness Events

A Discussion of Captain Kennedy's Historical Narrative, and ....

CAITHNESS EVENTS:

A DISCUSSION OF CAPTAIN KENNEDY'S HISTORICAL NARRATIVE,

AND

AN ACCOUNT OF THE BROYNACH EARLS.

BY

THOMAS SINCLAIR, M.A.,

AUTHOR OF " THE GUNNS," " THE SINCLAIRS OF ENGLAND,"
" TRAVEL SKETCH," ETC.

WITH PORTRAIT AND APPENDIX.

SINCLAIR ARMS.

WICK: W. RAE.
1894.

PRINTED AT THE
NORTHERN ENSIGN OFFICE,
WICK.

PREFACE.

In "Caithness Family History," by John Henderson, W.S., published at Edinburgh in 1884, there is reference on page 109 to "a MS. on Caithness affairs by the late Captain Kennedy of Wick;" and a letter to the *Northern Ensign* dated 11th November, 1882, mentions a statement by "a Wick gentleman, the late Captain Kennedy, who died many years ago," the same MS. the source of it.

Whether he was of the Kennedy wadsetter family of Stroma described by Henderson pp. 328-9, is an interesting question which may yet be solved. Murdoch Kennedy was the last of these semi-lairds of the famous island which divides the raging Pentland Firth; and his tenure closed, probably with his apparently eccentric life, about 1721. Dr. John Kennedy of Kermucks, Aberdeenshire, not Fifeshire, came to Caithness in 1659; or, at all events, in that year he had a wadset of part of Stroma, on which he built a house still existing, from George Sinclair, the sixth and neediest Earl of Caithness, Glenorchy's victim. Fleet-Paymaster John Bremner, R.N., a distinguished native of Canisbay, and a relative of the late James Bremner, C.E., Wick, remembers that local people used to say the first Kennedy was a buccaneer or pirate, and that he brought to Stroma a chest of Spanish doubloons, gold coins which have varied in value from 32s. to 64s., according to authorities. The reason of his wealth will appear, if the tradition had fact to go on; for it must have been the proceeds of the estate of Carnmux. Very little gold would count much then on the island. In a royal charter to Sir John Forbes, of date 4th August, 1669, John Kennedy, senior, and John Kennedy, junior, of Carnmux, Udny parish, Aberdeenshire, are mentioned among those who resigned portions to a newly-erected barony in favour of Sir John ; and the fact is given that John Moor was then the laird of Carmmux, otherwise spelt Kermucks. The elder John Kennedy came to Caithness after the family estate had been lost or sold, at all events, alienated. In 1643, 1644, and 1646 John Kennedy of Karmucks was on the committees of war for the sheriffdom of Aberdeen and a commissioner of supply, evidently the elder of the Johns. See "Acts of Parliament of Scotland." Bishop Robert Forbes's MS. diary of his visit to Caithness in 1762, says the latter was Dr. John Kennedy, and that he "fled to Stroma for homicide, having killed a Forbes of the family of Foveran." This throws some light upon Henderson's puzzle of three John Kennedys, for John "sometime elder of Kermucks" was "John elder of Stroma," two Johns being only in question. Murdoch of 1700 was brother of the younger John. The Canisbay parish register shows that the surname Kennedy has been prevalent since their time in the island. A minute-book of sasines of Caithness has various references to the Kennedy family. John Kennedy, younger, of Upren, in 1678 was put in possession of four penny and an octo of land in Stroma, his legal agent William Smith. On 1st April, 1681, at Wick, John Kennedy, elder, of Stroma, had sasine on Milton there, Donald Harper his lawyer. At Wick, 1st May, 1685, Patrick Sinclair, public-notary, presented to the court the sasine of John Kennedy of Carmucks, and of his spouse, on the nether township of Stroma. John Forbes, notary, of date Wick, 28th June, 1687, presented a sasine by John Kennedy, senior, of Stroma, in favour of John Sinclair of Ratter, his spouse, and children, of the over township of Stroma, and on 30th August another to Elizabeth Sinclair, the lady of Ratter, daughter of Sir William Sinclair of Mey, and her children, on the same land ; a renunciation by Beatrice Stuart, spouse to John Kennedy, younger, of Stroma, in favour of Elizabeth Sinclair, as to the over township, presented the same day. On 9th December, 1714, Hugh Campbell, public-notary, presented at Wick a sasine in favour of Murdo Kennedy, to the nether township of Stroma. Sutherland of Wester's tale about the Kennedy mummies in Stroma is too well known to need repetition ; the medical title of the first of the family in the county, perhaps explaining and excusing his son Murdoch's extraordinary filial or unfilial performances, charnel-house and dissecting-room apt to destroy reverence for the human form divine. Pope of Reay, Pennant, and Calder (pp. 19, 20) write of the Kennedys, Low noting the duel.

Of Captain Robert Kennedy, the author of the curious and valuable MS., a good deal can be gathered. He is written down "Major Rt. Kennedy" on the back of his little work, but the caligraphy is not his, and the "Major" must be a mistake of some one who possessed the document after his death. There is an endorsation in still another hand upon it thus, "To be returned to Wm. Waters, Savings Bank, Wick." In Wick church-yard an epitaph gives reliable facts :—"Sacred to the memory of Captain Robert Kennedy, 94th regiment, Scotch brigade, who died at Harland, 28th February, 1818, aged 65 ; likewise of his partner in life, Emilia Taylor, who died 27th November, 1834, aged 73." He was thus born in 1753 ; and as the MS. states within itself that it was composed at Wester in 1814, Captain Kennedy was 61 when he wrote it. That his wife was one of the Taylors of Thura, for whom see Henderson's work, is established. The parish register of Wick has several notices of him from 1799 to 1812 as witnessing and cautioning, where he appears as "Captain Robert Kennedy, Wester." On 22nd October, 1808, Donald Miller, tacksman of Noss, contracted to Jean Sutherland, Olrig, the cautioners Captain Robert Kennedy and Benjamin Waters, tacksman, Harland, the marriage cele-brated 10th November. In Olrig register "Mr." Donald Miller in East Noss, Wick, and "Miss" Jean Sutherland's contract is entered as at Olrig on 20th October, as if there had been a double. They were the parents of the late Kenneth Miller, London, a rich Australian merchant, married to Caroline Dunnet, Thurso. When "Lieutenant Robert Kennedy in Wick," he had a son born by his wife Emilia Taylor November 21st, 1800 ; but this son was not baptized till 15th November, 1818, as Benjamin Miller Taylor, the witnesses Bailie William Mackay and "Mr." Donald Miller, Staxigoe, the latter the father of Alexander of the Field (1740-1833), one of the founders of Wick herring fishery. At the time of that baptism Allan Macfarlane was the fishery officer, the ancestor of the Macfarlanes of Caithness. It would seem, from the above interval of birth and baptism, that Lieutenant Kennedy was of the Baptist persuasion, then prevalent in and about Wick, Sir Wiliam Sinclair of Keiss one of its notabilities. Indeed, Sir William had a son with the first name of Kennedy, as had also a John Sinclair, Gansclett, one of the Broynachs. But these facts may be out of connection with the captain. Earlier still, December 31st, 1790, Lieutenant Robert Kennedy and Emilia Taylor had a son baptised Patrick, the witnesses "Mr." Alexander Miller, Staxigoe, and "Mr." James Thomson. At that time they do not seem to have been Baptists. On April 10th, 1791, Lieutenant William Macbeath in Reiss and Jean Taylor baptized a son William, the witnesses Sir Benjamin Dunbar, Baronet of Hempriggs, and Lieutenant Robert Kennedy. As Jean must have been Kennedy's wife's sister, and as she is noted by Henderson as daughter of George Taylor, laird of Thura, married to Lieutenant Macbeath, it may certainly be taken that Mrs. Robert Kennedy was of the family. Jean was born 12th May, 1765, and died 19th June, 1846, her husband of the 91st regiment. More of these Macbeaths were officers in the army. In Canisbay parish register it is recorded that Lieutenant William Macbeath and "Mrs." Jean Taylor, daughter of George Taylor, Esquire of Thura, were lawfully married at Warse on 15th February, 1789. Her brother William was baptized 24th January, 1771, the witnesses Alexander Sinclair of Brabsterdorran and George Mackenzie, Thurso. There are several entries in Bower register about the Taylors.

It is evident that Captain Kennedy was of good standing; and the period in which he wrote this MS., entitled, "Anecdotes partly authenticated and partly traditional relative to the history of the county of Caithness," had special advantages to make his narrative peculiarly useful. There is no time with less knowledge of local affairs than that which his adult life covered, say from 1770 to 1818; and the lost events of the latter half of the eighteenth and beginning of the nineteenth century, must have been to him of everyday familiarity. It is a little to be regretted, therefore, that he seems to have had more interest in ancient facts than those near to him, unless his narrative stopped of necessity; but his piece is nevertheless well worthy of preservation, as it also deserves careful correction and kindly discussion as a county work. The text is scrupulously kept apart from the historical editorial commentaries upon it, in full justice to its author, by different type and other indication.

The story of the preservation of the MS. is that Bailie Waters, Wick, who was married to a daughter of Captain Robert Kennedy, left it, with other curiosities, to the late George Macadie, at the recent sale of whose effects it was purchased. It came into the hands afterwards of Rev. John Horne, 228, Meadowpark Street, Glasgow, the writer of the booklet, "Wick: In and Around it," a native of the town he describes. To him the editor of the MS. owes the opportunity of offering it, with full notes, to readers, as a considerable addition to the local literature. That during postal transmission the original went for some weeks astray, or into hiding, makes its safe keeping henceforth by book a subject of satisfaction, more especially to the sender and receiver.

By far the most important section of the following pages, however, is what to the Kennedy survival takes the form of a "continuation," chronological and substantial, embodying the latest results of exhaustive inquiries about the false succession of the earldom since 1772.

The appendix bears a large burden both of home and of transatlantic affairs.

THE PRESS CLUB,
LONDON, 1894.

CONTENTS.

CAITHNESS EVENTS.

CHAPTER I.

THE KENNEDY MANUSCRIPT'S OPENING.

" FROM the earliest accounts handed down to us, it would appear that Caithness and the neighbouring county Sutherland were possessed by a tribe of the people called Catti, who had emigrated from Germany, and that part of it which forms the present landgraviate or electorate of Hesse. The county of Caithness being a promontory advancing into the North Sea, and the word ness the general term for any projecting headland, as the Buchan ness, Orford ness, Fife ness, and others, it hence acquired the name of Caith ness, or the ness of the Catti. Whether these German adventurers were the original settlers, how long they possessed the district, or under what form of government, are points on which we have little information. Nor perhaps is it very material. But there can be no doubt that on the final subjugation or expulsion of the Picts by Kenneth Macalpin, the whole kingdom of Scotland to its utmost northern extremity became subject to that monarch."

The arrival of the Catti in Scotland is dated A.D. 91, during the reign of the Emperor Domitian. Agricola the Roman general was then conquering even to the Orkneys; and the Scottish king, Galgacus, whom the historian Tacitus has immortalized, received these Catti or Saxons, when they came to the river Tay, as valiant supporters against the "lords of the world." Their principal men became the rulers of North Scotland, taking first the surname of Murray and afterwards of Sutherland from their particular lands, the original name of the tribe surviving in the word Caithness. Tacitus described them in their fatherland as by far the bravest, most disciplined, and wisest of the Germans. As matter of fact, they were the section of the Teutons which history has called the Danes, and at an earlier period the Saxons, founders of the Anglo-Saxon kingdoms of England. Crantzius traces the Saxons to the Catti as ancestors, while Mercator and Carion make the landgraviate of Hesse, a word which is the synonym for Catti, the homeland of the tribe. Sharon Turner in his "History of the Anglo-Saxons" places the Catti on the shores of the German Ocean between the rivers Ems and Weser, but there is little doubt that they extended widely on all sides of what is now the great city of Hamburg on the river Elbe. That lowland shore is the cradle of all that has been greatest in English, Scotch, Irish, and American history. The Emperor Augustus fought there with the Catti, and his son-in-law Drusus rivalled the second Cæsar in his conquests, reaching the Weser and the Elbe. Tiberius also sought laurels in the same distant scenes, though with less success. But Germanicus the son of Drusus repeated his father's triumphs, extirpation his watchword. In particular, he sent Cœcina to destroy the Catti. "His arrival," says Tacitus, "was so little expected by the Catti, that their women and children were immediately taken prisoners or put to the sword, Mattium the capital was destroyed by fire, and the open plains were laid waste." Scandinavian incidents, as told by Snorro and Torfaeus, illustrate the case of setting fire to houses chiefly of wood then as now. Armine was the native hero contending against those conquerors who gave no quarter. Germanicus was recalled by Tiberius in A.D. 17, and the Roman arms never reached the Elbe again, though fighting continued in the southern parts of Germany. The Catti or Saxons learnt from the Romans the building of ships, and they were known to the Scottish shores even before their arrival in the Tay. That they increased greatly in power, as a confederation of Teutons, is locally illustrated by the fact that

Theodosius, who gained the surname of Saxonicus from his success, fought many battles by land and sea with them in the Orkneys, especially from A.D. 368 to 370. Claudian the poet's famous words refer to this, *Maduerunt Saxone fuso Orcades.* That the Orkneys could be bespattered with Saxon or Cattian blood, implies that the Germans were then the rulers of North Scotland.

But the conclusion must not be run to that they composed most, or even a large part, of the population there. Gibbon in his "Decline and Fall of the Roman Empire," chapter xxv., after discrediting some fabulous colonies, continues, "The present age is satisfied with the simple and rational opinion that the islands of Great Britain and Ireland were gradually peopled from the adjacent continent of Gaul. From the coast of Kent to the extremity of Caithness and Ulster, the memory of a Celtic origin was distinctly preserved in the perpetual resemblance of language, of religion, and of manners." He thinks the Scots were the men of the hills, and the Picts those of the plains. The latter had the name from the carnivorous highlanders of *cruitnich* or wheat-eaters, being agricultural, Aberdeenshire retaining most marks of them. These sections of Celts were the true *aborigines* or natives, and their subterranean houses, called *tumuli* or tullochs, attest to this day their low civilization and meagre economics. The Kimmerians, whom the Roman consul Marius overthrew B.C. 102, the earliest Celts known to European history, dwelt, Strabo and Ephorus said, in subterraneous dwellings called argillas, communicating by trenches; and in the British, Welsh, or Cymry language *argel* is a "covert." Burrowing in imitation of rabbits was, next to cave dwelling, the most primitive condition of human existence.

Over savages authentically cannibal by the evidence of Jerom, vol. ii., p. 75, which Gibbon accepts as veracious, it was good policy for a king of Scotland to place comparatively civilized leaders and governors like the Catti, who have long since amalgamated with the original Picts, as they were, in Caithness and the Orkneys. Claudian says that Theodosius "warmed Thule [or Shetland] with the blood of the Picts;" and Pacatus states that the Saxons were "consumed in naval wars" at the same time; so that the combination of the Catti with the Picts, or Saxon with Celt, is clear, as against the Romans, in that fourth century. At the beginning of the fifth century the Picts and Scots together attacked South Britain, on the Romans withdrawing to defend themselves against Alaric, King of the Goths. The Latinized and civilized Britons defended themselves as well as they could from 410 till 449, when they employed Hengist and Horsa, who had arrived with three Saxon cyules or vessels in Kent. These leaders effectually stopped the Irish (as the Scots are called by Turner) and the Picts, not improbably the heads of the northerns being also Saxon Danes, Greek thus meeting Greek. The chiefs of clans have long been considered of Norse origin, from their tall stature, light colour of eyes and hair, with other physical and mental peculiarities not Celtic. Mixture of race was and is, however, an omnipresent fact in all parts of this kingdom. Till Kenneth the Second's reign, the son of Alpin, North Scotland was under the Catti rulers, who had become Picts to all intents and purposes by blood and language, much as Englishmen have been transformed into Irishmen. His reign covers from A.D. 834 to 854. In 839 the great struggle for supremacy between the two Celtic communities of Scotland was bloodily settled in favour of the Scots; the Picts, as far as Orkney and Shetland, thoroughly subdued. Kenneth Macalpin ruled from Hadrian's wall to the Orkneys, according to George Buchanan the historian. But new expeditions of the Danes or Catti made the conquest of no value, the Scandinavians gradually re-occupying the whole of the islands and much of the mainland of Scotland, till 1263, when the defeat and death of King Hacon of Norway and the accession of his son King Magnus gave back some power again to the Scottish kings, though under tribute and homage. What the Catti were, how they governed Caithness, and for what time, can be gathered from such considerations to some true historical extent.

One of the most striking rounds of the wheel of life is to be seen in the fact that the ancestors of the Sinclair Earls of Caithness, when they were Earls or Princes of Orkney and Barons of Roslin Castle, Edinburgh, were also Dukes of Oldenburg in Westphalia, the exact homeland of the adventurous Catti. The duchy is now a part of the German empire, but in these Sinclairs' time belonged to Denmark, the principality acquired by them through a marriage with the Princess Florentia, daughter of the king of that country. On the Continent a duke is not, as here, a noble merely, but a crowned sovereign. One of these Dukes of Oldenburg was Prince Henry Sinclair, who was installed in the principality of the Orkneys and Shetlands in 1379, by Haquin, King of Norway and Sweden, in succession to his father and grandfather, and was the accepted second person of those kingdoms. Henry is now known to have been the first civilized discoverer of America, about 1390, a century in anticipation of Columbus, some of the true Catti in his sea company. Of his standing as Prince of Orkney there is a curious but absolute proof in Gibbon's "Decline and Fall of the Roman Empire." Martin V. was elected pope in 1417, three years before Henry died in grand old age, by the five nations of Christendom. France maintained that England, Ireland, Scotland, etc., ought not to be counted one of the five, but the learned priests of Britain argued with success at Rome the right to equality. Their chief argument, to quote Gibbon, was that "including England, Scotland, Wales, the four kingdoms of Ireland, and the Orkneys, the British islands are decorated with eight royal crowns." The then ruler of the Saxon Catti in Oldenburg thus wore a second crown for the Orkneys. As these German Danes were the founders of the Anglo-Saxon politics, their intimate relationships with Caithness have not only local but universal importance.

In William Guthrie's "State of the World," 14th edition, 1794, it is said, under the heading, "His Danish Majesty's German Dominions," that "in Westphalia the King of Denmark has the counties of Oldenburg [population then 80,000] and Delmenhorst [near Bremen], about 2000 square miles. They lie on the south side of the Weser. Their capitals have the same name. The first has the remains of a fortification and the last is an open place. Oldenburg gave a title to the first royal ancestor of his present Danish majesty. The country abounds with marshes and heaths, but its horses are the best in Germany." Christian VII., born in 1749, was the reigning king of Denmark and Norway, married to Carolina Matilda, the unfortunate sister of his Britannic majesty George III. There is a famous silver antique drinking vessel in the Royal Museum at Copenhagen, weighing about four pounds, called *Cornu Oldenburgicum*, "the Oldenburg horn," which tradition says "was presented to Otho I., Duke of

Oldenburg, by a ghost. Some, however, are of opinion that this vessel was made by order of Christian I., King of Denmark, the first of the Oldenburg race, who reigned in 1448." Torfæus the historian dedicated his "Orcades" to his patron Christian V. in 1697, whom he described as King of Denmark, Norway, of the Vandals and the Goths, Duke of Sleswick, Holsatia, Stormaria, and Ditmersch (districts near Hamburg), and "Earl in Oldenburg and Delmenhorst," so that the last two had reverted from the Sinclairs to the the Danish royal family.

Captain Kennedy, it will be seen later, refers to the Oldenburg and Delmenhorst duchy being held by the ancestors of the present Earl of the Catti. William Sinclair, the famous Earl of Orkney, Chancellor of Scotland, and the first Earl of Caithness of the surname, created so in 1455, was the last Duke of Oldenburg. King James III. of Scotland, who reigned from 1460 to 1488, married Margaret, Princess of Denmark; and by purchase, exchange, pensioning, and other means transferred from William all his Norwegian rights; a process which had been also going on, especially with reference to Orkney and Shetland, during the reign of the king's father, James II. William's daughter, Lady Catherine, was married to James the Third's brother, Alexander, Duke of Albany; and this family connection must have aided the royal purposes of Denmark and Scotland.

Enough, however, of digression from the MS., though few productions, in spite of essential value, need more of amplification and of bringing up to the modern mark of accuracy, founded on available histories, records, and other staple evidence. Of this the next chapter affords a notable example, the captain's limited means of knowledge more than an excuse for his artless honest errors.

CHAPTER II.

A BISHOP'S DEATH.

"The Harolds and their successors of Danish or Norwegian descent were possessed of the lowlands of the county long after a regular and permanent church establishment had taken place in Scotland, of which the following tale is illustrative. The Bishop of Caithness having by many and repeated acts of great oppression incurred the general odium of the inhabitants of his diocese, they applied for redress to the Earl. He, either not inclined to give himself much trouble in the matter, or perhaps unwilling to come to any rupture with the church, told the complainers that he would take no concern in anything that related to their Bishop, and they might boil him if they pleased. Glad at having thus obtained what they were willing to construct into a sanction for signal vengeance, which they meditated against the Bishop, the ferocious and infuriated populace proceeded immediately, in a body, towards the episcopal palace at Scrabster, near Thurso, the Bishop's ordinary residence. Having learned, however, on their way that he had gone to Wick some days before, on a visit to the Vicar, who lived there, they turned back and proceeded thither. The Bishop, who was on the road homewards riding through Sibster attended

only by his servant, observed this disorderly troop coming
forward to meet him.   He instantly rode off full speed to the
right, towards a place since called Kilmster, or 'kill minister,'
thinking by changing his course to have avoided meeting this
band of desperadoes.   They, however, having observed and
pursued him, he alighted from his horse at a farm house, and to
save his life, which he knew was aimed at, took shelter in a
kind of hiding hole with which most houses in those days were
provided.   It is still, or was very lately, to be seen communicating from the house to the corn-yard, under which it extended
for a considerable distance.   Here his savage pursuers detected
him and killed him, cutting his body in pieces, and boiling it,
thus carrying the hint dropped by the Earl into execution to
the letter.

" The barbarous murder thus committed on a person of such
high dignity in the church, stirred up, as may very naturally
be supposed, the whole clergy of the kingdom to bring their
complaints to the foot of the throne, and to insist on the most
exemplary and condign punishment being inflicted on all the
perpetrators and abettors of so horrid and sacrilegious an out-
rage.   Many disorders also having about that time taken place
in different parts of the kingdom, but more especially in the
north as being farthest removed from the scale of justice, King
William the Lion [who reigned from 1165 to 1214] found it
had become necessary to make a personal progress into those
distant parts, for the punishment of the guilty and restoration
of order among his subjects.   Accordingly, having collected a
sufficient force, he commenced his journey, redressing grievances

and punishing offenders and rebels on his way north, till he at
last arrived at the extremity of the kingdom.　Having reached
Caithness A.D. 1198, he took up his residence in Wick, and
directed all the Harold connection to be convened before him
on a certain day at Kilmster.　On a strict inquiry into all the
circumstances of the bishop's death, they were condemned to
the worst form of personal mutilation, the sentence executed at
once on the spot.　As further penance and atonement, they
were ordained to build a steeple to the church of Wick.　The
field in Kilmster where the trial was held and these bloody
transactions took place is to this day called the King's Field or
King's Stead.　It adjoins the farm house.　The steeple of Wick
was built by the punished Harold party, and continued standing
till the middle of the eighteenth century.　Having fallen into
decay, the rain penetrating many parts of the building, it gave
way at the foundation on a Sunday morning, tumbling with a
tremendous crash to the west.　The bell, which was of very
fine tone and long used thereafter by the church, came to the
ground on the outside of the churchyard, without sustaining
any material damage.　A small bit was broken out of the lip of
it, which injured the sound little or nothing.　On building a
new church lately, this bell was exchanged for another, not
nearly so good, though of much larger dimensions.　Effectual
and radical measures, as above, were taken for extinguishing
the Harold race."

The want of record references, and also of the ordinary historical
books, is manifest in Captain Kennedy's narrative; but, none the less, he

B

has added strange details of some transactions of the past. It seems that another bishop still of Caithness must be added to the two already known to have been killed by violence, and that the scene of the death was a few miles from Wick as described, the connection with steeple-building suggestively corroborative. Tradition may possibly have mangled established history to its own impressions, and the "kill-minister" theory is not reassuring, Kilminster meaning "church glebe." After stating what is known of murdered bishops, some judgment may be arrived at as to whether the Kilminster tale had footing.

George Buchanan in his "History of Scotland," book vii., cap. 49, says that a rumour of the death of King William the Lion had raised commotions, and "Harold, Earl of Orkney and Caithness, enraged with the Bishop of Caithness because he believed that the prelate had been decrying some of his demands from the king, seized him and deprived him of his eyes and tongue. The king destroyed most of the forces of Earl Harold in several battles. He hanged by his executioner their leader, after putting out his eyes, having been taken in flight, and all his male offspring he gave over to be emasculated. He fined in great sums of money the relatives and committers of the crimes. These things are narrated by Boethius, and confirmed by common report. A hill preserves the memory of the transactions, by taking its name from the emasculation." The date he gives is 1199, which practically is the same as Kennedy's. Another quotation from Buchanan proves mixing of events by the manuscript :—"In the year 1222, the Caithnessians having entered the sleeping-chamber of Adam their bishop, slew by night his chamber-servant, a monk, whom he had as companion, according to his manner, for he had formerly been Abbot of Melrose. They burnt himself, grievously wounded and dragged into the kitchen. The whole house they set in flames. It is said that the reason of such cruelty was that the bishop exacted tithes more oppressively than usual. The perpetrators being sought after diligently, were subjected to the heaviest punishments. The Earl of Caithness, though he was not present at the deed, was suspected of connivance. Afterwards, however, at a Christmas feast he obtained an assurance of safety from the suspicion at the king's hands."

In section viii. of "The Genealogy of the Earls of Sutherland" there is what seems to be a paraphrasing of Boethius thus:—"Harold, surnamed Chisholm or Guthred, the Thane of Caithness, accompanied with a number of scapethrifts and rebels, as the history calls them, began to exercise all kinds of misdemeanours and outrages, which savage people incensed by want and hatred ordinarily do, invading the poor and simple with cruel spoilings and slaughters. These rebels having ranged and raged through Caithness, and not satisfied with what they had done there, turned to Sutherland. Earl Hugh nicknamed Freskin defended, whereupon Harold returned to Caithness. Offended with John, Bishop of Caithness, for asserting the liberties of the church and for preventing him from obtaining portions of the bishopric which he had asked from the king, Harold seized Bishop John, pulled out his tongue and his eyes, and then killed him most inhumanly and cruelly. King William coming out of England A.D. 1198, and hearing of this barbarous fact, pursued Harold with his accomplices to Duncansbay, and apprehended them. He commanded exact or talion justice to be done." Harold had the corresponding retaliations to suffer, and was publicly hanged thereafter. Sir Robert Gordon repeats the tale of Boethius about the extinction of the whole Harold lineage, with the left-hand unsatisfactory evidence of the hill's name, where the unspeakable mutilations are supposed to have been executed. Bishop Adam, who wrote several books, succeeded Bishop John, Pope Honorius III. confirming his bishopric in 1218. He was murdered in 1222. "The inhabitants of Caithness," says Gordon, "conducted by the sons of Simon Harbister, nothing daunted by the late exemplary punishment, at the command of Magnus, their earl, entered the chamber of Bishop Adam in the town of Hackrick in Caithness, under silence of night, because he had excommunicated them for not paying their tithes. First they murdered a monk who was his companion. Then they haled and drew the bishop by the hair down to his kitchen, and there scourged him with sticks. Last of all they put fire to the house, and burnt the bishop in it. King Alexander II. who was at Jedburgh, hearing of the execrable fact, hastened north into Caithness with all speed to punish the offenders. After great search they were found and taken, to the number of 400, whom the king had publicly hanged. The whole lineage were mutilated, a strange kind of punishment twice inflicted upon the inhabitants. The earl having escaped was forfeited of land and dignity, but he came humbly to the king the third year after, 1225, on Christmas festivity, and was pardoned." Sir Robert in his sanctimonious prejudiced vein continues, "This Magnus, Thane or Earl of Caithness, was slain as he lay in bed by his own servants, whom he had oppressed and roughly treated. The house also wherein he was killed was set on fire and burnt over him, that the fact might seem to have chanced by some sudden adventure." Then he moralises about the pardon of man not being sufficient.

Sir Robert's colour to these events is only to be rightly seen by examining his lying "Short Discourse," written in 1630, magnifying the Gordons and trying to belittle the Sinclairs. He begins by quoting himself as above, adding that Harold was the son of Mac-William, and then he abridges the narrative about Bishop Adam's slaughter, stating gratuitously that Magnus, whom he takes care to call thane as if in depreciation, was used by his servants "after the same manner that he had caused the bishop to be used." His object was to prevent his contemporary, George, fifth Sinclair earl of Caithness, from claiming precedency over the earls of Sutherland by descent, male or female, from Earl Harold or Earl Magnus. The humour of the situation is that the Gordons as earls of Sutherland were only from 1515, and that they are believed to have been usurpers of the rights of the original Sutherlands, first in the person of Adam Gordon of Aboyne. Impostors are always impudent, and Sir Robert's theories attest the saying.

Torfaeus has carefully detailed, especially from Norse sources, the stories of the two bishops; and, on the whole, he is the best authority, though writing as late as 1697. After describing the battle between the two Harolds in 1196, around what is now called Harold's Tower, near Thurso, where the slain rival was buried; the expedition of Reginald, Lord of the Isles, by royal command against the conquering Harold, who was born in 1134; an establishing of six Scottish prefects over Caithness for King William the Lion, in other words, for the crown; the historian recounts the re-appearance of Earl Harold from Orkney with a huge army before Thurso, to recover what he believed was his county, partly as belonging to the Norwegian kingdom, then quite an intelligent position to assume. Besides, the two Harolds were relatives, and rivals on that score ; King William having really no right to the annexation of the lands and returns. The people of Thurso had been leaving their original Norse sympathies, and going over to the Scotch, to the disgust of Earl Harold, who though his father was Maddad, Earl of Athole, had northern rights from his mother Margaret, the Countess of that Perthshire earldom, half-sister of Earl Paul of Orkney and Shetland. When Earl Harold arrived in the bay of Thurso the townspeople were panic-stricken, and on his landing his troops, sent John, Bishop of Caithness, from the Palace of Scrabster in the neighbourhood, to pacify him and obtain pardon for the town. "When," says Torfaeus, "with a great attack the whole troops rushed out of the ships into the town, the bishop coming in front, the earl received him with mocking speech and laughter, and ordered him to be seized, and to be deprived of his tongue and eyes." It is not possible to avoid believing that the bishop had been active in the Scottish interest. Thurso surrendered, some were heavily punished, others fined, and the county, of which this was then the town, compelled to swear loyalty. The goods of the six king's prefects were confiscated, who fled to the court with complaints, the king promising to reinstate them double, with all speed. Soldiers were levied over Scotland, and King William the Lion, accompanied by the prefects, led a large army to the north, to oust Earl Harold. A huge encampment was made in the valley which lies between Sutherland and Caithness, now called Ousdale. The site of the camp extended from the top to the bottom of the vale, so numerous were the troops. Earl Harold, though he collected 7,200 men to oppose, gave up the attempt as hopeless against such a force, and sued for peace. After negotiations and Harold's consultation with the Caithness people, it was granted, on the condition of paying into the royal treasury one-fourth of all the goods of the county, as a fine for the death of the bishop, whom Torfaeus, however, did not believe to have been slain by Earl Harold, as other historians say. The king accepted Harold as earl of Caithness exactly on the same footing held by the younger slain Earl Harold.

In Rymer's "Foedera" there is a note that when Edward I. of England's commissioner examined the registers of the king's treasury of Scotland in 1282, one of the documents was "a quit-claim of the lands of the bonders of Caithness for the slaughter of the bishop." The Norse word bonders for farmers implies the earlier periods; but it is possible that this is the slaughter of Bishop Adam in 1222, and not of Bishop John in 1198; though the fact that Earl Harold had the Caithness bonders bound to pay the royal fourth, as above, nearly settles the point of the violent death of John against the impression of Torfaeus, even if his acuteness is seldom at fault.

Of his usual wisdom no better example can be brought forward than his treatment of the emasculation story, so gloated over for selfish purposes by Sir Robert Gordon. He urges that the contemporary Norse writer from whom he himself narrates says not a word of it. If he had known of it Torfaeus thinks he would not have omitted it, and that author is plainly silent. A Danish word *eista* is given as the origin of the falsehood. Ousdale was then known as Eysteindale, and a hill on the side of its valley Eystein Hill; hence a double and most erroneous meaning, not to say detestable. Eystein is the same as the well-known personal name Augustine; and Augustine's Hill is the full for Sir Robert Gordon's Stony Hill. Nothing is more borne in on one than that, with close study of history, and especially of its record and original monuments, very hideous atrocities become fictional, grounded on some accident of words, or on mere invention, to satisfy love of wonders. That a civilised monarch like William the Lion, fresh from the court of England, surrounded by the learned priests and gallant nobility of Scotland, could in the face of Europe, and Christian Europe as represented by the pope, order corporal mutilation of the primitive savage kind, is impossible to believe. Boethius is the first author of the tale, and Robertson and all others who read him for historic purposes admit his credulity to have been notorious. Posterity was deceived, Torfaeus contends, by likeness of words; for the valley where the king measured out his camp gave the Eystein or *eista* name to the neighbouring hill. It is well to be rid of this nightmare from Caithness history, and gratitude to Torfaeus is more than due for finally giving the

last blow to an infamous libel, not only on the county but on a gallant
king.

It would be rash to assume that no deed against the church, in the
person of one of its officials, was done at Kilmster; though Hackrick,
meaning Halkirk, has certainly the doubtful honour .of being the scene of
boiling one bishop. The "Codex Flateyensis" is used by Torfaeus in his
"Orcades" for the facts of this incident. After the death of John, Bishop
of Caithness, whom Earl Harold deprived of eyes and tongue, Bishop
Adam succeeded, born of unknown parents. He was found an infant
exposed at the door of a church. His unusual rigour in exacting tithes
displeased the people. The fault, however, was commonly thrown on a
monk, his chamberlain. Custom held that those who possessed 20 cows
through Caithness paid 20 marks of butter. He ordered the same from 15
cows, then from 12, and lastly 10; thus doubling the tithes, to the disgust
of the folk. They appealed to Earl John, not Magnus, as Gordon says,
who refused to mix himself up with their strife, but admitted the oppression.
The bishop was in Hakyrkia, whether so-called from a noted church or
because it was an estate of the church, *i.e.*, Thorsdale, or the valley of
Thurso river; and Rafn, the highest judge of the province, was his guest.
Earl John lived near in Brawl Castle. On a hill in the neighbourhood the
farmers held a meeting, and sent the last word to the bishop. Rafn, the
sheriff of that time, pointedly advised remission of the latest demands of
tithes, but the bishop said the mob would bridle itself soon, sending a
message meanwhile for soldiers from Earl John as protection. But it was
too late. A marshalled band attacked the house, running with full speed
from the meeting on the hill. Rafn, who was drinking wine with the
bishop in an upper room, recommended an immediate compromise. The
monk, however, going out, was at once struck across the face, and killed
near the door. When the bishop was told, he said the deed ought to have
been done sooner, for it was his chamberlain who had caused discord
between him and his people; and he sent a message of reconciliation to
them by Rafn, the judge. The more prudent were delighted with the
proposal, but the foolish, prompted by ferocity, seized the bishop on coming
out to make peace, led him into a small house, burnt it with torches, the

flame so sudden that those running to his help were powerless. His body was found little burnt in the house, and was buried with much ceremony. Alexander II., son of William the Lion, when told by the bishop's friends, was so enraged that the severity of the punishments exacted will never go from the memory of man, by slaughters, limbs cut off, confiscation of goods, proscriptions, and banishments. The monk was named Serlo, and had been of Melrose. Of the double martyrdom, as it was called by the church, the date was 13th September, 1222.

Torfaeus says Boethius and Demster repeat the emasculation legend in the story of the second as of the first bishop; so that it was evidently a "property," in the theatrical sense of this word, as the starving in dungeons of heirs by cruel fathers or uncles was the tale of scores of castles. Honest and learned investigation dissipates most of such unnatural inventions of the horrible.

In the fourth chapter of Calder's "History of Caithness," second edition, 1887, there is a popular account of these events; pp. 136-7 of "The Gunns" notice them; and the "Orkneyinga Saga" may be also consulted. Further discussion of the slain bishops will come at a later point more appropriately.

CHAPTER III.

THE CHEYNE FAMILY.

"THE mountainous or highland part of Caithness, by far the most extensive, was possessed at a very early period by a famous chieftain called Ronald Cheyne, while the northern and eastern portions along the sea-shores were under the dominion of the Danish or Norwegian Harolds, also at the same time earls of Orkney. Ronald Cheyne was the Nimrod of his day, and built many castles or seats in the highlands of Caithness, the ruins of which are still visible, to which he occasionally resorted for the convenience of hunting and fishing. Among others, he had a castle at the east end of Loch More, where the river of Thurso issues from that lake. Here he had a chest or kind of cruives so curiously constructed that, as the current of the stream was made to run through the chest, when a salmon dropped into it, his fall into the chest occasioned a bell to ring within the house, which gave instant notice to the chief and his attendants that their provision was secured."

Of the Cheynes a great deal is extant, not the least problematical, but supported by state and other sufficient record. Like the Sinclairs, they came from Normandy to England, and then settled in Scotland. Inverugie Castle, Aberdeenshire, was their home before coming to Caithness, where

Oldwick Castle became their chief residence, considerable ruins of which still exist near the modern Pulteneytown. Of the two Ronald Cheynes it is the later, the last of his line, that Captain Kennedy refers to as of county hunting fame. Sir Robert Gordon, p. 54, after stating that he lived in the time of William Sutherland, the earl who died at Dunrobin in 1370, continues thus :—" Ronald Cheyne, a Caithness man, was during his time a great commander in that country. Of him many fables are reported among the vulgar sort of people, and chiefly concerning his hunting, in which he much delighted. Doubtless the Cheynes had at one time many possessions and were of the greatest command and power in that country, but they were never the earls of it. All the lands belonging to this Reginald Cheyne were divided among his daughters, which disposition was ratified by the charter of confirmation of King David Bruce [that is, David II., who reigned from 1329 to 1371]. One of Ronald Cheyne's daughters was married to Nicholas Sutherland, Earl William's brother, with whom he had the Cheynes' third part of the lands of Caithness and the third part of the lands of Duffus in Morayshire, becoming thus the laird of Duffus, which property his posterity enjoys to this day [1630]." On page 140 of " The Gunns " there is the knowledge that the ruins of Ronald's hunting lodge at Loch More were used to build a bridge there over the Thurso 150 years ago ; and that the nurse who secreted his two daughters from him, lived with them in a cottage in the corrie or glen on the east of Dorrery Hill.

In his Introduction, p. xxv., Henderson says, " From 1290 to 1350 the Federiths, a Morayshire [?] family, held extensive possessions in Caithness. How these were acquired does not appear. Contemporary with them, and allied by marriage, were the Cheynes, one of whom, styled in charters Ronald, Lord Cheyne, obtained a grant from William Federith of Federith [Aberdeenshire] of a fourth part of Caithness, which was confirmed by David the Second. The possessions of the Cheyne family were scattered over the various parishes in the county ; and on the death of Reginald Cheyne, the one half passed to the Sutherlands, afterwards of Duffus or Dove-house, through the marriage of one of his two daughters and heiresses to Nicholas, brother of the Earl of Sutherland, and the other half to the

Keiths, afterwards the Earls-marshal of Scotland, by the marriage of the other daughter to John Keith of Inverugie about 1380." He adds that the Keiths fell heirs thus to Ackergill estates, and the Sutherlands to Oldwick Castle and Berriedale.

The *Celtic Magazine* of 1880-1 has many useful details, some of them from Dr. Skene's "Notes on the Earldom of Caithness" in the F.S.A. Scot. prints. Sir Reginald Cheyne of Inverugie Castle had two sons, Reginald, Lord Chamberlain of Scotland in 1267, and Henry, appointed Bishop of Aberdeen in 1281. Freskin Murray had half of Caithness, his only children Mary and Christina, by his wife Johanna, who died before 1269; and the two heiresses had therefore a fourth each. Mary married Sir Reginald Cheyne and Christina William Federith. By some arrangement Federith and his wife gave their fourth to Cheyne, who thus secured the half of the county, with the Castle of Oldwick head messuage.

Nisbet says in his "Heraldry" that Reginald Cheyne, father, and Reginald Cheyne, son, were parties with the rest of the magnates of Scotland who resolved in 1283 that Margaret, "the fair maid of Norway," was their queen. Sir Reginald and other Cheynes swore fealty to Edward I. of England in 1296, Reginald having been present at the convention of Brigham in 1289. In the Scottish rolls or papers long kept in the Tower, London, and now in the Record Office there, it is stated that King Edward I. gave a present of 10 deer to Reginald Cheyne, the father, and 6 to Reginald, the son; the deed of gift dated Thirsk, Yorkshire, 23rd August, 1291. These English deer may be represented in the northern stock of to-day. The father was then sheriff of Inverness, the sheriffdom reaching to Pentland Firth, and in 1292 the roll of his accounts in that office is mentioned as produced. When arranging the government of Scotland in 1305, Edward I. appointed Sir Reginald one of the justiciaries in the north beyond the Grampian mountains. He died before 6th November, 1313, leaving his properties to his son Reginald, the hero of the Kennedy MS., and the last of the males of his branch. He was a warrior and statesman as well as a hunter. Dr. Burton mentions him as one of the signers of the letter to the pope by the Scotch nobility from Arbroath Abbey, 6th April, 1320, asking favour for the Bruce dynasty. At the battle of Halidon Hill, so fatal to the Scots, he was taken prisoner, but soon released. He married a Norsewoman, and had two daughters only, of whom everyone knows the romantic story. Educated at the convent of Murkle, near Thurso, Marjory married in 1337 Nicholas, brother of the Earl of Sutherland, and Mariotta wedded John Keith. The last Sir Reginald was called in Gaelic *Morar na Shean*, that is, Lord Cheyne. He died very old about 1350, and was buried in the Abbey of Olgrimore, Halkirk parish, covered with sand brought by his wish from the strand of beloved Loch More, " the big lake."

How the Cheynes came to Caithness is indicated by the following from Robertson's " Index ":—" Charter by David II. to Reginald Cheyne of the fourth part of Caithness, in the county of Inverness, given by William Federith ;" and again, " Charter by King David II. to Marjory Cheyne of the lands of Strathbrock, Linlithgowshire, and half of Caithness."

Rymer's " Foedera " has a treaty between Scotland and Wales by which they were not to make peace with the English king, Henry II., except after mutual agreement. It is written in Latin, and dated 18th March, 1258, thirteen Scotch earls and lords putting their signatures and seals to it, among whom were Reginald Cheyne and Freskin Murray. The Scotch and Welsh meanwhile were to have free trade for their merchants. Rymer has also the full text of the obligation of 1283 by the Scottish nobles, referred to in Nisbet's " Heraldry," to make the Maiden of Norway, Margaret, the daughter of King Eric and of Margaret, King Alexander the Third's sister, their queen ; Reginald Cheyne, the father, and Reginald Cheyne, the son, among the signatures. It is a Latin document, dated Scone, 5th February, 1283. Both the Cheynes signed the letter of the people of Scotland, or rather of their earl and baron representatives, consulting Edward the First of England as to a marriage between his son Edward and the Maiden of Norway. It is written in Norman-French, and dated Brigham, the nearest day after St Gregory's, 1289. The Maiden was Queen of Scotland from 1286, though absent in Norway. At the convention at Norham, near the Borders, when King Edward I. was deciding between the claimants to the Scottish throne, the Cheynes, father and son, were electors and nominators in favour of John Baliol, who was appointed king. The two Reginalds are so mentioned in a list of 5th June, 1292.

In the chartulary of Moray appears, "Mary, spouse of Reginald Cheyne, lord of Duffus, daughter of the deceased Freskin Murray." She is the supposed mother of Reginald *filius* or *fitz*. There is, however, a document in the "Foedera" about the widows of Scotland which would go to show that the senior Reginald was married, secondly, to Eustachia Colville, and she may have been the great hunter's mother. Translated from Latin it runs, "The king to the sheriff of Ayr, salvation. Because Eustachia, who was wife of the deceased Reginald Cheyne, is at our peace, and has given the oath of fidelity to us, we order you that if it is clear to you that the said Eustachia was wife of the beforesaid Reginald, and that the same Reginald died before the alliance entered into and contracted against us between John Baliol, lately King of Scotland, and the King of France and his brother Charles, and that Eustachia has not been married afterwards to any of our enemies, then the lands and tenements which Eustachia held before the confederacy, as well those in dowry as those of her own heredity, in the beforesaid kingdom and land, up to the day in which we caused those lands and tenements to be taken into our hand, you must make to be restored and delivered without delay to the same Eustachia, together with the crops on those lands and tenements. The castles and fortalices of Eustachia, if she has such, are, however, to be retained to the command of the guardian and keeper of the land and kingdom of Scotland. With the king witness, at Berwick-on-Tweed, 3rd September, 1296." This king was Edward I., the "hammer of the Scots;" and he sent similar letters to the sheriffs of Banff, Kincardine in Mearns, Forfar, Aberdeen, and Inverness in favour of Eustachia, who had estates in all those sheriffdoms. There is an apt notice in the "Encyclopædia Britannica," ninth edition, in the article "Heraldry," of the rich relict:— "Eustachia Colville, widow of Reginald Cheyne in 1316, bore a cross moline, square, pierced for Colville, between four crosslets fitchy for Cheyne." A seal gives this knowledge of the Cheyne arms. Various references raise the question whether there were not three Reginald Cheynes in succession, a common enough repetition of a first name in baronial families.

Edward the First's orders to the sheriffs show that, though the

Cheynes swore fealty to him in 1292, they changed sides, and had their lands consequently confiscated, the restoration to the widow full proof. In a charter of the year 1336 by Edward III. of England, Reginald Cheyne and William Federith are described as that king's "Scottish enemies;" but whether this hostility may not point to an earlier date is a problem, the Bruce dynasty then established long on the throne by the war of independence, of which Bannockburn battle was the final solution in 1314. Consistency in patriotism was hardly possible at all for the nobles during that period of false or indefinite rivalries for the crown. In a "Calendar of Documents about Scotland," the originals in London Record Office, several notices help to show the changes. On 19th February, 1303-4, peace was notified by Edward I. to Lord Reginald Cheyne by letter, to "the men of Inverness," then including Caithness, and to various leaders. When Bruce was getting the upper hand, Cheyne was still on the side of the English; for Edward II., on setting out for Boulogne, in France, addressed messages, of date 13th and 14th December, 1307, to the clergy and nobles of Scotland, begging the former to keep peace there, and the latter to be obedient to John of Brittany, Earl of Richmond, warden or guardian, Reginald Cheyne one of those thus called to duty. On May 30th, 1308, Edward II., from Westminster, thanks Reginald Cheyne and ten other Scots for their faithful service to him and his father. But towards the end of that year most of the Scotch, if not all, swore fidelity to King Robert the Bruce.

It is easy to list the Caithness lands of the Cheynes, through the accounts in state records of their subsequent possession by Lord Oliphant and the Sinclair earls. They had portions or all of Sibster-Brawl, Greystone, Assery, Claredon, Borland-Murkle, Sordale, Aimster, Ormlie, Thurdistoft, Sibmister, salmon-fishing of Thurso river, Shurrery, Brawlbin, Skaill, Borrowston, Lybster, Stangergill, East Murkle, Duncansbay, Dunnet, Wesbuster, Barrock, Ratter, Corsback, Reaster, Holland, Tister, Brabster-dorran, Oldwick, Canister, Sarclet, Ulbster, Thrumster, Stemster, Humster, Thurster, Bilbster, Ackergill, Reiss, Harland, Wester, Mirelandnorn, and the town of Wick. See "Origines Parochiales Scotiæ," "The Oliphants in Scotland," and the national printed records. What the Cheynes had in other counties was of large extent and value.

Of Henry Cheyne, Bishop of Aberdeen, there is some account in Bishop Pococke's "Tour through Scotland in 1760" when describing that town :—"Bishop Henry Cheyne having taken part with the Comyns [now Cummings] in the dispute about the crown, on their being worsted, fled to England. But when things were settled he was very acceptable to King Robert Bruce. Out of the arrears due to the see, he built the fine Gothic bridge of one arch over the Don, 72 feet wide and 60 feet high." The editor, D. W. Kemp, notes that Henry Cheyne was the nephew of John Comyn. In Machar Cathedral, Aberdeen, Pococke says "the arms of the bishops and benefactors are blazoned with their names;" and among the monumental inscriptions on the north side, Henry Cheyne appears as the eleventh bishop. It is his bridge that Lord Byron dreaded to pass as a boy, Balgounie Brig, because of the superstition that it was to fall with a widow's son on it. Duncan's "Itinerary of Scotland," 1822, says that a mile from Aberdeen the Don is crossed "by Bishop Cheyne's majestic Gothic arch, built 1329. The height from the water to the top of the arch is $34\frac{1}{2}$ feet, the width 62 feet 10 inches. At ebb tide the water is 20 feet deep." The same useful guide-book notes that "about one mile from the church of New Deer stands old Castle Fedderatt, once a place of considerable strength," the home of the Federiths, twenty-eight and a half miles from Aberdeen.

There is a Wick memorial of a Cheyne in an epitaph of the churchyard thus, "Here lies a famous and honest man named David Paton, some time master of the household and chamberlain to George, [fifth] Earl of Caithness, who departed the 19th November, 1640, his age 82. Here lies also Janet Cheyne, his spouse, who departed the 7th September, 1639, her age 80. D. P., J. C." More Cheyne lore could be collected, but the Kennedy MS. paragraph is already overweighted, and with a direction to what Calder's second edition of the "History of Caithness" tells of those gallant Normans, the captain's narrative is resumed.

CHAPTER IV.

KEITH AND GUNN FEUD.

"About the middle of the fifteenth century, the clan Gunn resided principally in the mountainous district between the counties of Sutherland and Caithness. They were a species of Swiss, who, in the frequent disputes between the inhabitants of these counties, hired their services to the highest bidder, and were in nowise remarkable for having the strictest ideas as to *meum* and *tuum*. They happened to incur the enmity and resentment of Earl-marshal Keith, and many skirmishes had taken place with various success. At length they agreed to decide all their differences in a field in the vicinity of Innocents' Chapel, commonly called St. Tears' Kirk, situated between Castle Girnigoe and Ackergill Tower. There 200 horsemen of each clan were to meet, and either conclude a peace or fight it out. On the day appointed, in the year 1478 [some make it 1434 and others 1464], the 200 of the clan Gunn having first arrived, under the command of Coroner Gunn, had alighted from their horses, and were waiting the approach of their antagonists, the Keiths. On these coming up, it was perceived that there were indeed only 200 horsemen, but that each had a foot-soldier mounted behind him. Seeing themselves outwitted and outnumbered, and sensible that in this dilemma they had little quarter to expect from the inveterate malice and rancour of their enemies, the Gunns betook themselves to the neighbouring chapel for sanctuary. This availed them nothing, for the Keiths, having broken open the doors, entered, and massacred every man of them at the foot of the altar. See ' Conflicts of the Clans.'

" The Gunns, thirsting for revenge of this treacherous and inhuman slaughter of their clan, agreed among themselves, some time thereafter, to waylay the Earl-marshal Keith on a journey out of the county. Having obtained intelligence of the time of his departure, as well as of the exact number of which his retinue was to consist, they resolved to meet him on a bleak moor near Clyth, in the parish of Latheron ; but scorning to imitate the ungenerous advantage which had been taken of themselves on the former occasion, they determined that their number should not exceed those who were to attend the earl. William McHamish, however, grandson of Coroner Gunn slain at St. Tears' Chapel, ordered that four of their best and picked men were to be selected to single out and engage the earl-marshal himself, whom they called the *Keach More* or the Big Keith, a man of huge stature and proportional strength of body. This precaution was no more than necessary, for when the parties met, and the engagement began, the *Keach More* made such good use of the formidable weapon he wielded, which was the two-handed claymore, that he despatched his four picked antagonists besides many of inferior note. He was on the point of gaining the day, in a great measure owing to his own

D

personal prowess, when an unlucky back stroke from the broad-sword of one of the clan Gunn, who lay wounded on the field. having divided the main tendon of his leg, he was thus put completely *hors de combat*. Having been helped to his horse, he made his escape to the south, with only a very few of his attendants. The rest of them, after his lordship's own discomfiture, were all hewn in pieces by the enraged Gunns, who had become masters of the field of battle. Considering their honour vindicated and revenge gratified, the clan Gunn proceeded to the burial of the dead of both parties on the scene of action, which is clearly pointed out, even to this day, by some scores of large flagstones, set up in regular rows, and fixed deeply and perpendicularly in the ground. One of these stones is said to be placed at the head of the grave of each warrior who fell in the obstinate and sanguinary combat.

"It has been supposed that the earl - marshal never returned to Caithness after this fight, and that he transferred his lands in it to his grandson, John Sinclair, the third Earl of Caithness, either by sale or deed of gift. Those lands, as well as the manorplace of Ackergill Tower, now [1814] the seat of Sir Benjamin Dunbar, baronet, were purchased by Sir William Dunbar, great-grandfather to Sir Benjamin, from the Earl of Breadalbane, who in the latter end of the seventeenth century had, by an adjudication deed of sale or otherwise, obtained possession of the whole of the estates of the then Earl of Caithness."

The number 200 instead of 12 in the massacre by the Keiths makes Captain Kennedy's a new version of the dread tale, which need not be further discussed, as its various points have appeared in "The Gunns," published in 1890. On the question of its exact date opinion still differs. Sheriff Æneas Mackay, LL.D., in the ninth edition of the "Encyclopædia Britannica," article "Scotland," is inclined to fix the massacre as in 1434. About that time James I., the author of "The King's Quire or Book," an English poem, had put down the terrible feuds of the Highlands. Some years previously the clans Chattan and Cameron had nearly exterminated each other; and the Keith and Gunn episode may have been a resurgence of the suppressed evil, the king's energetic presence at Inverness in 1427 having created civil order in the north. His murder at Perth in 1437 let loose clan strife again, and next year the Mackays from Strathnaver attacked Caithness, defeating its people in The Chase of Sandside. That year of 1438, the Mackays aided the Keiths to gain the battle of Tannach Moor, near Wick, over the Gunns. It would seem certain that the event at Innocents' Chapel took place after this, but to accept absolutely either Calder's date of 1464 or Kennedy's of 1478 is still dangerous. Sir Robert Gordon says, after describing this very battle of Tannach, "All these seditions and troubles, which happened at that time, not only in the diocese of Caithness but also throughout the whole kingdom, fell out through the division which was then in the state between the governor, Sir Alexander Livingstone, and Sir William Crichton, chancellor of Scotland, after King James the First's death, during the minority of James II., from 1437 until 1443." Sheriff Mackay's 1434 is too early, as being when the rule of James the First was most dreaded by disturbers of his peace.

The battle of Mannistones, at the home of the present and previous Earl of Caithness in Mid Clyth, was, according to Captain Kennedy, the last conflict between the Keiths and the Gunns, and therefore subsequent to the tragedy at St. Tears' Chapel. The date of 1478 might be applicable to that fight, which has memorial in the name of a stream near where it took place, The Red Burn, the water of which was said to have been tinged with the blood shed on that day.

As to Earl-marshal Keith never returning to Caithness after the fight of Mannistones, it may or may not be true, but that he gave his lands there away is not fact, for "Origines Parochiales Scotiae" says the castle of

Ackergill, with half the lands, was in 1538 possessed by William, Earl-marshal, as probably the other half was also. It was through buying Lord Oliphant's estates that the Sinclairs secured Ackergill, the Oliphants succeeding the Keiths. In 1547 there was violent fighting between George Sinclair, the fourth earl, great-grandson of the *Keach More,* for possession of Ackergill Castle, "belonging to William, Earl-marshal," but soon after Earl George's. In Blaeu's "Atlas Major," published 1662, there is a "New Description of Caithness," written some years previously, with this about the castles, "Castle Sinclair, formerly Girnigoe, the castle of the Sinclair earls, not far from the town of Wick, holds the first place. In its neighbourhood is Ackergill, not long ago belonging to the family of the Keiths, but now devolved upon these earls." In the same essay it is added, "Keith of Invernigie, from the marshal's family, holds much property here. The illustrious earl-marshal heired it not long since, the head of the house of Keith. They gave it over by writ to the Mowats." Enough is said to show that the *Keach More* did not give his Caithness lands to his grandson, John Sinclair, third Earl of Caithness ; though Earl John must have had portions through his Keith mother's dowry, and from her third part, if she was a dowager. In the charter-chest of the extinct laird of Mey family, so-called "Earls of Caithness," there was a charter of Ackergill, given by Lord Oliphant on 7th May, 1550, to George Sinclair, the fourth earl, justiciary of Caithness and Sutherland. The deed of entail by Sir William Dunbar of Hempriggs, 11th October, 1707, which will be published in full in the "Bruce-Caithness MSS.," gives complete account of how the Dunbars, really Sutherlands, came into possession of Ackergill and the rest of their valuable estates. Two purchases from John Campbell, first Earl of Breadalbane (the Glenorchy of Altimarlach battle), and from his son John, one dated 12th August, 20th September, and 31st October, 1691, and the other 6th and 23rd November, 1699, were the introduction of the Sutherlands into Ackergill Tower as its lairds, Sir Benjamin becoming Lord Duffus, a peer, who died in 1843.

CHAPTER V.

THE SECOND SINCLAIR EARL OF CAITHNESS.

"THE dignity of the earldom of Caithness was conferred on George Chrichton [8th July, 1452, who died in 1455]. As his patent was limited to the heirs male of his own body, and that he died without such issue, the earldom became extinct, and the title remained dormant till revived the same year of 1455 in William Sinclair, Earl or Duke of Orkney. His second son William, by Marjory Sutherland, daughter of John, Master of Sutherland, had the resignation of the earldom from his father in 1476, on which resignation King James III. gave him a charter under the great seal dated 7th December, 1476. At the battle of Flodden he was slain with King James IV. in the year 1513, the second Earl of Caithness of the surname of Sinclair. The Sinclairs had Orkney long before then, and one of them, Henry, was also Prince of Oldenburg and Delmenhorst on the continent of Europe.

"William, second Earl of Caithness, had by some means or other incurred the displeasure of the king to such a degree that he could not venture to appear at court, and proceedings had even been commenced against him for the forfeiture of his estates

and titles. However, on the general summons being issued in
1513 for all the nobility of the realm to attend the king in the
war with England, he assembled his whole clan, and having
clothed them in a handsome and splendid green uniform,
marched on a Monday morning at their head out of the county,
crossing the famous pass called the Ord the same evening on
the way to join his sovereign. Upon their arrival at the
appointed rendezvous, which from the great distance they had
come occurred only the evening before the battle of Flodden,
this gallant troop attracted his majesty's particular notice.
Having enquired who they were, the principal people about
him, who were well aware of his resentment against the Earl of
Caithness, showed backwardness in telling him. But the king
insisted on knowing, and was at last informed that it was the
earl, at the head of the clan Sinclair. His majesty, struck
with this unexpected example of generous loyalty and obedience, after musing within his own mind for a little, is said to
have expressed himself thus, 'My lords, since that is the case,
let byegones be byegones, for a friend in need is a friend
indeed.' Having sent for the earl, he freely forgave him his
former trespasses, and ordered a full pardon and remission to
be instantly made out. But as there was no parchment to be
found in the camp, the king ordered it to be written on the
head of a drum, and having signed the document in presence of
his nobility, directed it to be cut out from the drum. Thereafter he delivered it, with his own hand, to Lord Caithness.
His lordship, uncertain of the result that might arise from the
ensuing day's work, and sensible of the importance of such a

valuable document, took the prudent resolution of despatching a
trusty messenger home with it to Caithness that very evening.
He acted wisely, for on the next day he and all his followers,
after exhibiting repeated proofs of the most unexampled and
determined gallantry and bravery in the unfortunate field of
Flodden, were all at last cut off to a man. The messenger
having arrived in safety, the parchment was lodged in the
archives of the family of Caithness, where it still remains. The
severe and almost wholly fatal blow which the clan had thus
met with, made such a deep impression that, until very lately,
no gentleman of the name of Sinclair was inclined to cross the
pass of the Ord on a Monday, nor was there any one of that
surname who did not prefer a coat of any other colour than
green.

"This William, the second of the Sinclairs who held the
earldom of Caithness, resided at Castle Girnigoe, situated on a
projecting rock or precipice near Noss Head, on the east side
of Sinclair Bay. From the ruins of this castle still standing,
it was not only a mansion of great strength, but also, for those
days, of considerable elegance of architecture. He was married
to Mary Keith, daughter to the laird of Inverugie, Aberdeenshire, afterwards earl-marshal of Scotland. The earl-marshal
was possessed of lands in Caithness, and resided frequently at
Ackergill Tower, a very strong keep at the most inland part of
Sinclair Bay, about a couple of miles west of Castle Girnigoe.
He was possessed of property throughout the whole north of
Scotland, and it is said that when he came occasionally from his
chief seat of Dunottar Castle, in the Mearns, to visit his estate

in Caithness, he could during the whole course of his journey lodge every night in a house of his own.

" Having quarrelled with his son-in-law, the Earl of Caithness, he took an opportunity, on a New Year's day morning, when the Earl of Caithness and some attendants had been out coursing with greyhounds, and were returning on horseback within bowshot of the battlements of Ackergill Tower, to wound him with an arrow, which stuck in the back of his neck. Finding himself wounded, the earl did not attempt to withdraw the arrow, but, having clapped spurs to his horse, arrived at his own house of Castle Girnigoe. His lady enquiring what sport he had met with, he replied, ' Not much ; only, in passing by Ackergill Tower, your father sent home a New Year's gift for you, which you may find fixed in the back of my neck.' "

Earl William was immediate younger half-brother of William, Lord Sinclair, Ravensheuch Castle, Fifeshire, who was declared on 26th January, 1488, by the king and parliament of Scotland, "chief of that blood." Sir Oliver Sinclair, baron of Roslin Castle, Edinburgh, was Earl William's full younger brother. Their sister Catherine was the Duchess of Albany, her husband Alexander Stuart heir-presumptive to the crown and second person in the kingdom. Stoddart in his "Armorial Bearings," Edinburgh, 1881, states that the mullet was borne long in the Roslin arms, and that as this was the mark of cadency of third son, Sir Oliver's position in the family was so settled, though there has been some disputing as to his juniority or seniority to Earl William. In the rolls of parliament surviving, this earl is entered 16th February, 1505, one of many such entries as a legislator. At the parliament in Edinburgh on 8th June, 1504, he witnessed a document by the Earl of Athole promising to underlie the law for treason. In the 1505 roll mentioned, he is one of the four earls in that particular list. See "Acta Parliamentorum Scotiae." His father is mentioned on 26th July, 1515, as "a noble and powerful lord, William, Count of Caithness," in a Latin paper about his daughter Catherine's divorce for too near consanguinity, proof that her brother Earl William was the second holder of the dignity. In the charter of the great seal mentioned by Kennedy he is described as son of William, Earl of Caithness, and Marjory Sutherland, his countess, Marjory's third part of the earldom expressly reserved.

During the latter part of the second Earl William's life, Caithness was in great disorder. In 1503 parliament passed an act saying, "Because there has been great lack and fault of justice in the north parts, as Caithness and Ross, for fault of the want of division of the sheriffdom of Inverness, to our regret, and these parts are so far distant from the burgh of Inverness, through which people cannot come speedily there by reason of the great expense, labour, and travel, and therefore great enormities and trespasses have grown, in default of officers within those parts who have power to put good rule among the people, etc., etc." On these grounds there were to be a sheriff of Ross and one of Caithness, the latter sitting at Dornoch or Wick as convenient. In the work entitled "Parliaments of Scotland," covering 1357 to 1707, it is said that this act, though passed, was inoperative till ratified for Caithness in 1641 and Ross in 1649. It is evident that it was an invasion of Earl William's rights as justiciary over what is now Sutherland and Caithness. There is evidence that he was in trouble, if not forfeiture; but, from the above, actual deprivation at any time did not result.

The extraordinary thing is that the Kennedy MS. seems to throw light on what may have been the cause of his antagonism with the crown. A bishop slain at Kilmster by the earl's men, for which he as justiciary was made responsible, according to the legal habits of the time, would appear to be historical fact. Captain Kennedy attached to the event what he gathered from Gordon and others about the earlier slaughters of bishops, and thus went far astray, though preserving the incident, for which he deserves all praise. Mackay in his "History of the Mackays" quotes from an old inventory a remission by George Hepburn (uncle of the first Earl of

E

Bothwell), who was Apostle or Bishop of the Isles from 1510 to 1513, in favour of William, Earl of Caithness, " for all murders and crimes committed by him for the year 1501 to 1510." Of course, " murders and crimes " must mean incidents of disputed administration, feuds, and property quarrels, according to the language of the period, not personal felony at all. This ecclesiastical remission, shortly before Earl William fell at Flodden, was a prerequisite to his sovereign's remission on that fatal field. In the sasine or possessory document following his son John's retour in 1513, on his father's death that year, to the earldom, there is this referring to the remission, " Wherein the murder of the bishop is thought to be comprehended, of date 1510." Mackay supposes that a rivalry between Earl William's brother John and the bishop was the cause of the latter's slaughter. John Sinclair was Bishop-elect of Caithness, but was never consecrated, the pope refusing, it is suggested, at the instance of the ruling bishop. After the bishop's murder, it was Adam Gordon, the dean, who administered the bishopric, and not John. In 1503 Andrew Stuart is Bishop of Caithness, see " Acts of Parliament of Scotland ; " and it was not he who was murdered, because he appears in the same record at Perth in the king's council, 26th November, 1513, the year of Flodden. It was a predecessor, perhaps Bishop Prosper, whose life closed so wretchedly in the hole at Kilmster, and evidence survives to show that the bishop-elect, John Sinclair, was not at all events the prime cause of the slaughter, if even at all responsible. Kilmster was then church land, afterwards coming into the possession of the Caithness earls, with many other places there, all erected into a barony, with South Kilmster mansion the head messuage. Of the charters of the great seal, one was confirmed by King James III. at Edinburgh, 9th November, 1478, which had been granted by William, Bishop of Caithness, in 1455, with consent of the dean and chapter, to his brother, Gilbert Mudy. It gave him the castles of Scrabster and Skibo with 10 merks of land for defending the church lands, with the ninepenny lands of Wick, Alterwall, Stroma, and Dorrery. It was about these very properties Earl William's grandson Earl George. had such battling, and the quarrel evidently began in the grandfather's time. Alexander Gordon, Earl of Sutherland, held them and others in feefarm from the church before

Earl George. Enough is stated to show that the murder of a Bishop of Caithness, about 1470, must be added to the previous tragedies ; and not improbably he also brought vengeance, evidently in his case also of the people, on his own head by looking too much after lay interests, if it was not rivalry with the earl's brother, Bishop John, to whom he resigned the bishopric in 1460. A new fact among old records may quite clear up this all but lost chapter of the past. Earl William held the earldom for thirty-seven years from his father's resignation of it, but he must have been in possession much longer. His sole crime, in connection with the murder of the bishop, was that the tragedy happened in Kilmster within his jurisdiction bounds ; and the supposed or real forfeiture must have been because he did not punish the mob with the rigour which the church and the crown demanded. There can be no doubt that he was popular with Caithnessmen, as his gallant following to fight the English is brilliant proof. If the people had grievances against their bishop in the fifteenth as in the thirteenth century, there may have been good reasons for the earl's leniency, to himself most of all testing, as putting his life and fortune to the balance. James IV. apprised Canisbay, etc., from him for a debt of £400, another reason of discontent. John Leyden, the Border poet, has spirited lines about prowess on the field of Flodden ; but Earl William's "amber locks" did not "redundant wave," as they were very grey.

CHAPTER VI.

BATTLE OF SUMMERDALE IN ORKNEY.

" WILLIAM SINCLAIR, the Earl of Caithness slain at Flodden with King James the Fourth, was succeeded by his son John, whom he had by his wife the daughter of the earl-marshal. This Earl John having passed over to Orkney, with a view to recover lands to which he laid claim in that country, was treacherously set upon by the inhabitants, and slain with all his attendants, near the loch of Stennis, on the mainland of Orkney, in the year 1529. It is said those savage Orcadians were complaisant enough to send back his lordship's head to Caithness. Hence arose a custom of saying, by way of malediction to any one going on an expedition where no success was expected or even desired, ' I wish you as lucky a journey as Lord Caithness made to Orkney, his head being all that came back.' Earl John was married to Elizabeth Sutherland, daughter of Lord Duffus, by whom he had his second son and successor, George, the fourth earl."

Of Earl John, who was named after his uncle, Bishop-elect John, for whom the, as it seems, *fated* Bishop Prosper resigned, a good deal is now known. Sir Robert Gordon tells how he recovered the county of Sutherland and Dunrobin Castle from the Countess of Sutherland's supposed illegitimate brother, Alexander Sutherland, for Adam Gordon. He had a charter of Helmsdale in 1513, probably through his Sutherland wife, a near relative to, and of the same surname with, the countess, Adam's wife. In "The Statistical Account of Scotland," published in 1791, etc., there is information about the Orkney expedition, especially with regard to Earl John's gigantic follower William Sutherland of Berriedale. Sutherland had a just grievance against Robert Gunn of Braemore, who tricked him into marrying his sister, and he went to complain to the Earl of Caithness as justiciary. Earl John, who had previous troubles with Gunn (see notes to Calder, 2nd edition, p. 324), "promised him redress as soon as he returned from the Orkneys, where he was going to quell a rebellion, along with Sinclair, the baron of Roslin, and wished that William, being a very strong man, would accompany him. William consented to do so, and returned from Girnigoe Castle to Berriedale Castle, to bid his friends farewell before he would go so dangerous an expedition. Just as he was parting from them, at the burial ground on the east side of the Water of Berriedale, he told his friends that he suspected he never would return from Orkney. He then laid himself down on the heath, and desired his companions to fix two stones in the earth, the one at his head and the other at his feet, in order to show to posterity his uncommon stature. These stones remain there still, and the exact distance between them is 9 feet 5 inches. Tradition also mentions his height to have been above 9 feet. He went with Lord Caithness and the rest to the Orkneys, where he, as well as the earl and his son" [William, the eldest], "was killed. This happened in the year 1529. The cause of the rebellion was this. In the year 1529 King James V. granted the islands of Orkney to his natural brother, James Stuart, Earl of Moray, and his heirs male. The inhabitants took umbrage that an overlord should be interposed between them and the sovereign, and rose in arms under the command of Sir James Sinclair of Sanday. Lord Sinclair, baron of Roslin" [rather of Ravensheuch], "and John, Earl of Caithness, were sent with a party of men to quell the rebels, but the islanders defeated them, and the earl and his son William, with William More Sutherland, who accompanied them, were killed. The Caithnessmen who survived carried back the Earl of

Caithness's head, to be buried in his lordship's burial place in Caithness." The battle was fought 18th May, 1529, four miles from Stromness.

In March, 1529, Buchanan says King James V. gave James Stuart, Earl of Moray, the lieutenancy of the kingdom; and Orkney may have been part of his promotions at the time. Some Scotch historians say that it was John, Earl of Caithness, who was in rebellion against his king, trying to seize the Orkneys on old claims, but the above has a greater appearance of truth. It is said that the Caithness or king's party numbered 500. Worsaae, the Dane, agrees with "The Statistical Account" in writing, "The islanders took up arms under the command of their governor, Sir James Sinclair, to oppose the appointment of a crown vassal over them."

In the *Celtic Magazine* for 1887 there are many interesting points touched upon about Earl John; and "The Bruce Caithness MSS.," published in the *Northern Ensign*, have a charter by him of Ekirnoss to Alexander Brisbane of Reiss, dated Girnigoe Castle, 28th March, 1520. In Bain's "Merchant Guilds of Aberdeen" he gives a charter of donation to Trinity Convent, Aberdeen, for his father Earl William's soul, his own, and the souls of friends and successors, 264 masses to be sung yearly in all, the charter dated Wick, 19th October, 1523. His lawful brother, the Hon. Alexander Sinclair of Dunbeath, also benefited that convent or hospital of friars, rather monastery than convent. The register of the great seal has a confirmation by James V. to Earl John and his wife Elizabeth Sutherland on 14th July, 1527, of Keiss, Stone, and Rowdale; and he then resigned the earldom in favour of his son William, who was, however, slain at the battle of Summerdale in 1529.

CHAPTER VII.

JOHN, MASTER OF CAITHNESS, AND HIS FATHER.

" GEORGE, fourth Earl of Caithness, was married to Lady Elizabeth Grahame, daughter to the Earl of Montrose, by whom he had his eldest son, John, Lord Berriedale, commonly called John Garrow, the latter word meaning strong, rough, or robust. John was so named from his uncommon size and bodily strength. Earl George had several other children by his wife. George Sinclair was his third son, to whom he gave the lands of Mey, &c., from whom the present Earl of Caithness [James Sinclair, born in 1767, then 47, the first Mey usurper of the title from the Broynach lawful earls] and the greater part of all the gentry of the county of the surname of Sinclair are descended. George, the fourth earl, lived much at court, where he appears to have been in great favour. He sat as chancellor of the jury on Bothwell's trial. By interest he had his town of Wick erected into a royal burgh. He died at Edinburgh in 1583, where his heart was soldered up in a leaden box and conveyed to Caithness. There it was deposited in the family burial-place, a vault in the Sinclairs' aisle at Wick.

" Having conceived some grudge or umbrage against his son, John Garrow, he had him confined in a subterraneous vault in

Castle Girnigoe, under the custody of Ingelram or Ingram and David Sinclair, two brothers who during the earl's absence acted as factors or trustees for his lordship. These men, thinking they were doing an acceptable piece of service to their constituent, had treated John Garrow, his son, with the most unparalleled harshness and cruelty. The tradition is that dreading vengeance if he ever recovered his liberty, or tired at last with guarding him strictly, they concerted the following scheme for getting rid of him at once. His dinner, the only meal allowed, was every day carried down to him at a fixed hour, and being, as already said, a man of most uncommon health and strength, he indulged his appetite in eating heartily of such victuals as were set before him. They therefore, after having designedly omitted to send him down the regular meal one day as usual, sent him on the following day a large mess of salt beef, and, as a refinement on their ordinary cruelty, accompanied it with the covered, but this time empty, flagon in which he usually had his drink. The consequence was that on their next visit to the vault he was found dead, and the earl was written to that his son had died suddenly in confinement.

"This John Garrow had been married to Lady Jean Hepburn, daughter of the Earl of Bothwell. When he married her, she was the widow of John Stuart, Prior of Coldinghame. By her he had George, the fifth Earl of Caithness, James Sinclair of Murkle, Sir John Sinclair of Greenland and Ratter, and John Sinclair of Stirkoke, slain in a skirmish in the streets of Thurso in 1612. He had also a daughter, who was Lady Cowdenknows, and Henry Sinclair, a bastard son. George, the fourth earl, had, besides his eldest son, John Garrow, a second William, a third George above-mentioned, and a fourth David, who begat William Sinclair of Forss Mills and John Sinclair of Dunn [a pencilled note says 'William Sinclair was son of David Sinclair of Dunn']. Earl George had also four daughters, the first, Lady Barbara married to the Earl of Sutherland but had no issue; the second, Lady Agnes, Countess of Errol, afterwards married to Alexander Gordon of Strathdown, who had issue by both her husbands; the third, Lady Elizabeth, married to Lord Duffus, and afterwards to Huchcon Mackay of Farr; the fourth, to another Lord Duffus. He was likewise father to Alexander Sinclair of Dunbeath, a bastard, whose successors disponed the lands of Dunbeath to Lord Forbes, who again sold them to Sir John Sinclair, brother to the laird of Mey [a pencilled note says 'Alexander Sinclair was son of William, the second Earl of Caithness, and not a bastard,' about which fact there is no doubt whatever]. He had another bastard son who was parson of Olrig. [This Rev. William was the son of the deceased Henry, Lord Sinclair, and was legitimated 20th February, 1539, under the designation of Master William Sinclair, Rector of Olrig, for which see the register of charters under the great seal]."

Beside this strictly local account by Captain Kennedy of the supposed tragedy or tragedies of Girnigoe Castle, let the calumnies of Sir Robert Gordon, in all their naked virulence, be placed, as extracted from his "Genealogy of the Earls of Sutherland." On page 157 he says, "John, Master of Caithness, was punished by the hands of his own father, whom God in his just judgment had appointed to be his scourge, for burning the church of Dornoch, by famishing him to death in woeful captivity." On pp. 163-4 it is said that, "At this very time George, Earl of Caithness, became jealous of his eldest son, John, Master of Caithness, and suspected that he was plotting something against his life, by the assistance of Mackay of Strathnaver, who, to clear himself and the Master of Caithness from these imputations and surmises, persuaded the Master to go to Girnigoe Castle and submit himself to his father's will and pleasure. To this the Master yielded at Mackay's earnest entreaty. The very same night that they arrived at Girnigoe, now [1630] called Castle Sinclair, the Earl of Caithness, as he was talking with his son the Master, caused by a secret sign a company of men to rush in at the chamber door and apprehend the Master, who presently was fettered in sure bonds, and thrust into prison within that castle. There he was kept in miserable captivity for the space of seven years, and died at last in prison by famine and vermin, the disastrous subject of cruel fortune."

By the context, the opening phrase of the extract, "At this very time," could only mean between 28th August, 1571, and July, 1573; so that on Gordon's own statements, the Master was not imprisoned seven years, his gravestone in Wick recording the death as on 15th March, 1576. Other evidence proves the imprisonment to have been from September, 1572, arbitration documents in Barrogill Castle so showing. Gordon therefore doubles this fact, as he exaggerates everything on which his malice can found blame.

The story of the Master's killing of his brother William is the same class of lie, even judged on Gordon's narration. He says that Murdoch, the keeper of the prison, was detected by William in a plot to rescue the Master, and was hanged. He then commits himself to the following :— "The Master of Caithness, understanding how matters went, and that his brother William Sinclair had discovered the plot to their father, watched his time till he found his brother alone with him in the prison, being come hither to visit him, and then invaded and bruised him so with the irons wherewith himself was enchained, that he died within fifteen days thereafter." As if to enhance the absurdity of this false accusation of murder, or even of manslaughter, to disgrace the Sinclair family if he could, the

ridiculously untrue side-head is put to the passage :—" The Master of
Caithness straugleth his own brother to death." For if a struggle took
place at all, of which there is no indication beyond a bitter enemy's secret
writing in a private manuscript, it would hardly take fifteen days to
complete a strangulation ; nor, if one died that length of time after an
actual encounter, was it ever by the laws of any country considered more
than an accident. William, the forefather of the present legitimated
Ulbsters, fell sick in some ordinary way ; and the Gordon family of
Sutherland, as usual, made capital of scandal out of his decease, for hatred
of Earl George, whom they had wronged, it must be said, somewhat to
their cost, in his day.

On page 177 Sir Robert describes the earl as " the unnatural destroyer
and scourger of his own *children*," the transition from singular to plural
easy for the arrant liar. Two pages follow with imaginary evil designs,
which only Sir Robert's own devilish ingenuity created, on libellous
cowardly paper of 1630, the treachery printed in 1813. Earl George, he
says, caused John Gordon, Earl of Sutherland, Sir Robert's grandfather,
to be made away with, a doubtful tale of poisoning at Helmsdale Castle ;
and as guardian of the only son, Alexander Gordon, and only daughter,
Margaret Gordon, he was to marry the latter to his son William Sinclair,
and despatch Alexander, so that William should be Earl of Sutherland !
He was to kill the Mackay ruling family of Strathnaver, and make his third
son George Sinclair lord there ! His eldest, the Master, was to be made
justiciary of Sutherland and Caithness ! So go Sir Robert's evil dreams,
which answer themselves, the last " design " being surely very useless, since
the state records show the Earl and the Master of Caithness in possession
of the justiciaryship from Bonar Bridge to John O'Groats. Gordon was a
monomaniac in revenging what he foolishly considered his father Earl
Alexander's wrongs, inflicted by Earl George, the ward being the real
transgressor in breaking that legal relationship, universally accepted by the
lieges. He even gloats on the tale that in 1588 Wick was burnt by John
Mac-Gilchalm of Rasay, and the ashes of Earl George's heart, in a leaden
case, strewed by the cateran from the isles to the winds of heaven. As Earl
George died in 1583, the ashes must have been imaginary. It is not worth

discussing a madman's one idea, the bare extracts full proof of the insanity of his unreasonable malevolence, none the less that the Caithness family were near relatives by several ties to the Gordons. Stabbing in the back is nothing by way of treachery to his writing; excess defeating him, however, of his revenge with cultivated posterity, who cannot for a moment accept his monstrosities, himself the monster by trying to blacken established honour and renown with falsehood. That a statesman like Earl George, a constant member of the Privy Council of Scotland, then equivalent to what is now the Cabinet or Ministry, and a man versed as justiciary in the daily administration of civil and criminal law, should indulge in melodramatic "designs," is a mere superstition of the canting, cowardly, and cruel hypocrite that Sir Robert Gordon always becomes when he touches Sinclair themes. On other subjects he is sane and useful. The earl is vindicated with success from the historian's defamation in the *Celtic Magazine* for 1887, by a lawyer without personal prejudice of relationship or interest.

John Galt, the novelist, in his "Autobiography," vol. ii., p. 238, has this:—"The 'Entail,' which is supposed to be among the best of my novels, is founded on a family anecdote related by a friend. The characters are selected according to my own liking, but the tale is true, and except in incidental circumstances deserves to be considered a kind of history in private life. The sunny summer storm and shipwreck, described as con-summating the fate of the last heir of entail, were introduced to allow of a description of the northern coast which I received from Miss Sinclair, the daughter of the celebrated baronet. I never was myself near that part of the coast in which the scene is laid, but I have been frequently assured it is correctly given, as well as some other Highland circumstances alluded to in the book." The "Autobiography" of this Scottish novelist, Sir Walter Scott's reputed second, of wide European, Asiatic, and American travel and conversance in practical and political affairs, was published in 1833; and Miss Sinclair to whom he refers was Catherine, the novelist, daughter of Sir John of Thurso Castle, the agriculturist. As she was directly descended from William Sinclair, who is said to have been a victim of Girnigoe tragedy, so intelligent a family's traditions deserve special attention. Her communications about Caithness history are of a peculiar character, and demand place.

After bringing some of his characters to Wick, for sea-bathing and change of scene, Galt sets them to making little excursions in the neighbourhood, thus recounted :—" The objects they visited and the tales and traditions of the country were alike new and interesting to the whole party ; and it was agreed that before leaving Wick the gentlemen should conduct the ladies to some of the remarkable spots which they had themselves visited, among other places Girnigoe Castle, the ancient princely abode of the Earls of Caithness, the superb remains of which still obtain additional veneration, in the opinion of the people, from the many guilty and gloomy traditions that fear and fancy have exaggerated in preserving the imperfect recollection of its early history." Donald Gunn, "the worthy dominie of Wick," agreed to act as guide. "The party reached the peninsula on which the princely ruins of the united castles of Girnigoe and Sinclair are situated. The long grass on the bartisans and window-sills of the ruins streamed and hissed in the wind."

Their guide "related to them the mournful legends of those solitary towers. But although he dwelt with particular emphasis on the story of the bishop whom one of the Earls of Caithness [before the Sinclairs] had ordered his vassals to boil in a cauldron, on account of his extortions, their sympathy was more sorrowfully awakened by the woeful fate of the young [45] Master of Caithness, who in 1576 fell a victim to the jealousy of his father. At that time George the Earl was with his son the Master of Caithness on the leet of the lovers of Euphemia, the only daughter of an ancestor of Lord Reay. The lady was young and beautiful, and naturally preferred the son to the father. But the earl was a haughty baron, and in revenge for his son proving a more thriving wooer, was desirous of putting him for a season out of the way, but not by the dirk, as the use and wont of that epoch of rule might have justified. Accordingly, one afternoon as they were sitting together in the hall at yonder architraved window in the second storey, the wrathful earl clapped his hands thrice, and in came three black-aviced kerns in rusted armour, who, by a signal harmonised between them and Earl George, seized the lawful heir, and dragged him to a dampish captivity in that vault of which you may see the yawning hungry throat in the chasm between the two principal buildings. . . . . Soon after the imprisonment of his son, the earl being obliged to render attendance at the court of Stirling, left his son in the custody of Murdo Mackean Roy, who on the departure of his master was persuaded by the prisoner to connive at a plan for his escape. But the plot was discovered by William, the earl's second son, who apprehended Murdo, and executed him on the instant. Immediately afterwards he went down into the dungeon, and threatened his brother also with immediate punishment, if he again attempted to corrupt his keepers. The indignant young nobleman, though well ironed, sprang upon Lord William, and bruised him with such violence that he soon after died. David and Ingram Sinclair were then appointed custodiers of the prisoner, but availing themselves of the absence of the earl and the confusion occasioned by the death of William, they embezzled the money in the castle, and fled, leaving their young lord in the dungeon a prey to the horrors of hunger, of which he died. About seven years after, the earl, while he lamented the fatal consequences of his own rash rivalry, and concealed his thirst for revenge, having heard that Ingram Sinclair, who had retired with his booty to a distant part of the county, intended to celebrate the marriage of his daughter with a great feast, resolved to make the festival the scene of punishment. Accordingly, with a numerous retinue, he proceeded to hunt in the neighbourhood of Ingram's residence, and availing himself of the hospitable courtesies of the time, he entered the banquet hall, and slew the traitor in the midst of his guests."

It was not the Master's father but his son, also Earl George, who had connection with the death of Ingram; and the lady novelist's imagination has added other fictional touches, especially of the love kind, to the bare facts of history; but there are many marks of real knowledge in certain parts of what was thus transmitted down in the Ulbster house's traditions. Captain Kennedy's further narrative, illustrated by existing state records, will enable just views to be fixed at last about the so-called tragedies of Girnigoe Castle.

CHAPTER VIII.

REVENGE OR JUSTICE.

"George, the fifth earl, was sent abroad by his grandfather, and educated in Sweden, between which country and Caithness there was in those days a good deal of intermarriage and friendly intercourse, many of the name of Sinclair settled in Sweden ever since that period. One of their descendants was the unfortunate Colonel Sinclair, assassinated in Germany about the middle of the last century, while on a secret and confidential mission. See "The Annual Register" [1739]. On the death of George, the fourth earl, at Edinburgh, in 1583, his grandson and heir having returned from Sweden, and having taken possession of his estate and dignity, took a disgust to Castle Girnigoe as the scene of his father's tragical sufferings. He began to build the more modern and elegant mansion of Castle Sinclair in its vicinity, meanwhile setting up house at Keiss Castle on the opposite side of Sinclair Bay, whence he could see every day how his improvements at Castle Sinclair were going on.

"In the meantime Ingram and David Sinclair, who were well known to have treated the earl's father with great cruelty while he was under their charge, and were generally reported and believed to have put a period to his existence in the manner above related, had removed from Castle Girnigoe on the death of the old earl. In his employment it is said that they, and particularly Ingram, had amassed a very considerable sum of money, and had settled themselves, Ingram at Wester, two miles to the south of the young earl's residence at Keiss, and David at Milton, about a mile to the west of Wick. Whether it happened that there was no positive proof of John Garrow having been despatched in the manner reported above, or that the young earl for other reasons best known to himself declined any investigation into the circumstances of his father's death, notwithstanding his silence and his appearing to be in habits of friendly intercourse with the reputed perpetrators, he had in his own mind determined on ample vengeance.

"Some time after the earl had established himself at Keiss, Ingram Sinclair, the elder brother, who resided at Wester, had a daughter who was to be married, and some days before the marriage he asked his chief to honour them with his presence at the wedding, to which he agreed. On the morning of the wedding day, when the two brothers and their friends and relatives were assembled at Wester previous to the ceremony, and were waiting the earl's arrival, they observed him and his retinue coming along the links of Keiss. To show respect for his lordship, Ingram went down to receive and meet him at his crossing of the river, which is about three hundred yards below the House of Wester. The wedding folks were all left standing outside at the end of the house. The earl and his suite were mounted on horseback, and his lordship, according to the fashion of those days, had a pair of pistols of exquisite workmanship in his holster cases. He valued them much, and called them his black corbies or ravens. Ingram had seen the pair before on his visits to the earl's house at Keiss. On their meeting at the water side, after the ordinary compliments and while Ingram was walking up at his lordship's feet towards the house, the earl said to him, drawing out one of his pistols, 'What think you, Ingram? One of my corbies missed fire this morning.' 'I wonder much, my lord, at that,' replied Ingram, 'for they seem to be of a very superior kind.' 'I thought so too,' said his lordship, 'and shall be much disappointed if they fail me now, in inflicting punishment where it has been long and justly due.' At the same time he fired the pistol and laid the unfortunate Ingram dead at his horse's feet. The surprise of the company who beheld this scene may be more easily conceived than described. All took to their heels, or endeavoured to hide themselves as they best could, not knowing where a business thus begun might terminate. David Sinclair, the other brother, having instantly mounted his horse, took the road homewards to his own house at Milton; but, being hotly pursued by the earl and his attendants, was overtaken on the hill of Reiss, and despatched in a similar manner to what Ingram had been. Judging that he had thus appeased the *manes* or ghost of John Garrow, the earl after this returned deliberately along the sands to his castle at Keiss. Whether it was owing to the earl's superior interest, or to the general odium under which these unfortunate brothers had fallen for

F

their treatment of his lordship's father, it does not appear that any inquiry was ever instituted into the circumstances of their death.

" It has been said that at the instant of time when the scene was acted, the bride and her maidens were sportively amusing themselves, on the grass, examining and trying on the ring which was to be used in the approaching ceremony. In the alarm and bustle caused by this tragical and unexpected event, the ring was dropped to the ground by some one of them, and as may naturally be supposed was little thought of or enquired about at the moment. Be this as it may, certain it is that lately a very curious and antique hoop ring was picked up at Wester, in planting potatoes near this spot. It is of the purest gold wire curiously twisted together, the exact represen-tation of a serpent coiled into a circle with its tail in its mouth. This was the symbol adopted by the ancient Egyptians in their hieroglyphics for representing what was eternal or perpetual, a circle being from its nature without end. Such a figure for a wedding ring might very naturally be construed into an emblem of endless and perpetual love and affection. The ring is now [1814] in the hands of Captain Robert Kennedy, residing at Wester, and weighs something more than ten pennyweights, or value to nearly two guineas.

" There is a tradition current among the people of the district that, on the earl's return from Sweden, Ingram, fearful of being called to account for his intromissions with the old earl's affairs, and suspecting that he might in some forcible or short-handed manner be deprived of the money which he had gathered together during his administration, came to the resolution some time before his death to conceal it under ground. The soil for about five hundred yards to the westward of the House of Wester is corn land, at the extremity of which it is bounded by a rising ground, which intercepts the view from the house farther westward. It may be about two hundred yards more from the highest point of this ridge, which then slopes westward, to the edge of a deep and extensive moss. It is said that Ingram, having wrapped up his money in a raw hide, took the precaution of locking up his family and servants to prevent their discovering what he was about. From a hole in the barn door, however, he was watched by his man-servant going west, with his bundle on his back and a spade in his hand, till the rising ground prevented seeing how far he went. Judging from the time he had been absent, as well as from some moss which was observed sticking to the spade, it was concluded that he had gone no farther than the edge of the moss. It is very likely that Ingram's money lies there snugly, and perhaps may continue to do so until the last day. It is further said that every day after, until his death, he was seen taking a daily walk westward to the rising ground, in all probability to satisfy himself, without going to the exact spot where it lay, that his hoard was safe and undiscovered."

The register of the great seal authenticates and, to some degree, rationalises this tragical tale. King James VI. at Holyroodhouse, Edinburgh, of date 19th May, 1585, gave letters of remission for the deeds to George, Earl of Caithness ; James Sinclair, the Master of Caithness, his brother ; David their brother ; Matthew, son of the deceased David Sinclair of Dunn ; John, son of the deceased Mr William Sinclair, rector of Olrig ; Archibald, Thomas, James, George, and Alexander Hepburn ; George Manson ; William Manson or Rorison ; Donald Groat ; Donald Sutherland, son of Angus Hectorson ; James Paxton, servant of the Master of Caithness ; James and George Mullikin ; Thomas Manson, son of the deceased William Manson in Field ; John Hay ; John Waterston ; William Taylor ; Malcolm Alexanderson ; Edward Jameson, servants of the Earl ; and others, their comrades. The letters were to last for their lifetime, and freed them from all responsibility for, among other things, " art and part of the slaughters of Ingram and David Sinclair, brothers, in the month of February, 1584."

In a note to No. XII. of " The Bruce-Caithness MSS." this pardon is discussed, as well as some notices of Ingram Sinclair in the extensive contract of which that No. is composed. Sir Robert Douglas's " Peerage " is referred to for the date of Earl George's birth, namely 1565 ; so that he was about nineteen when these real tragedies took place. It is new that he spent some of his youth in Sweden, which even increases the similarity between his mission and Hamlet's, if he revenged his father's death. But the number of county gentlemen and ordinary individuals involved, suggests a fatal broil rather than his personal action, though as earl and justiciary he was technically liable for slaughter by his own company or by others. On no other grounds can it be understood that the king's pardon was so easy and so early, Scottish history showing numerous examples of punishment to life and forfeiture of lands for slaughter even by the highest nobles. Besides, Ingram was the laird of Blingery, now containing 261 acres arable and 2560 acres pasture, had tacks of the vicarages or tithes of Bower and Watten, held a wadset from Knappo barony, Wick, had been master of the household or chamberlain at Girnigoe Castle, and a person of such importance otherwise that his death could not be hushed up or overlooked in any way, even if it had not been accentuated by that of his brother David. Both of them were witnesses to the charter of Canisbay, etc., given to the young earl's uncle William, dated Girnigoe Castle, 1st March, 1572, Ingram adding to his name, " of Blingery." In the contract

MS. XII. already mentioned, of date Kircaldy and Girnigoe, 24th July and 30th December, 1595, to which George, the fifth earl, was a party, not only is the "deceased Ingram Sinclair of Blingery" mentioned, but also his heirs, Earl George promising to respect their rights as given by his uncle George of Mey. If Lord Maxwell was executed for the slaughter of a gentleman, to take an example, this same Earl George as justiciary delivering him up, though a relative, so stern was the law, to justice at Edinburgh, how could he have himself gone scot-free, if he had killed with his own hands, as Calder says too dramatically, these important brothers? Archibald Hepburn was the earl's master of the household when the events happened, and as Queen Mary's Hepburn, the Earl of Bothwell and Duke of Orkney, was Earl George's maternal uncle, the Hepburns perhaps were characteristically ready to revenge the death of John, Master of Caithness, husband of Lady Jean Hepburn. But probabilities need not be put, the incidents of a brawl quite enough to account for what is absolutely known of the historical facts and of their sequences. See the notes to "The Bruce-Caithness MSS." for further treatment, not only of these slaughters, but of the Master's decease in Girnigoe Castle, then the busy centre of the affairs of Caithness and Sutherland; his father the justiciary, and all deeds open to the criticism of a daily crowd, learned and unlearned, of an average at least up to 200 or 300. It is not in such a scene that judicial murder of an earl's heir could take place, at first or second hand, by salt beef, starvation, surfeit, or other mythical method; though the two brothers may, none the less, have been most blameworthy as guardians, and deserved their fate, in the unpremeditated way it seems to have overtaken them, putting melodrama to one side. The earl's brother James, at the fight a youth of seventeen, and then Master of Caithness, is the forefather of the Murkle and Broynach family, who are now heads of the house of Sinclair, and represented by James, the present rightful Earl of Caithness, aged 28, and unmarried.

About the Swedish Sinclair of "The Annual Register," there is very definite knowledge in the *Scots Magazine*, vols. i. and ii., especially a letter by the Czarina Ann, who reigned over Russia from 1730 to 1740, entered thus under the heading "Foreign History:"—"Her Czarian majesty very warmly resents the report about Baron Sinclair, who was carrying despatches from Constantinople to Stockholm, being murdered by two officers in Russian pay, and the following is the extract of an order from the czarina, dated July 3rd, 1739, old style, and sent to her ministers at foreign courts:—'We are very much surprised to hear of the rumour at Berlin concerning the murder of Sinclair, a Swedish officer, as if it had been committed by two of our officers. We have thought fit to order all our ministers at foreign courts to declare in our name that, so far from having any hand in, or any sort of concern with, so base an action, if it really was committed in the manner reported, we have an abhorrence of a crime so detestable. As it has been committed on the limits of Silesia and Lusatia, we have thought it necessary to request the Emperor of Germany and the King of Poland that they would please to order diligent search to be made for those malefactors, in order to punish them. But we cannot imagine that any of our subjects have so far forgot themselves as to do such an enormous crime. Yet we declare that we will use all endeavours imaginable to discover those criminals, and to give them exemplary punishment, in order to discover to the whole world how much we abhor such action, equally base and abominable, it being our intention to cultivate good harmony and friendship with Sweden.'

"The Summary of Public Affairs," has, "Sweden is at present a very divided kingdom, distinguished into three factions—one in the interest of their country; one in favour of Germany and Russia, which gives most uneasiness to the whole state; another obsequious to the dictates of a certain eminent political cardinal. After the death of Major Sinclair, affairs at Stockholm seemed to be greatly perplexed, and the preparations on the side of Finland have not been prosecuted with much vigour. The reader may not be displeased, in this place, with the inscription which his Swedish majesty has caused to be written on the tomb of the unfortunate Sinclair, in the church of St. Nicholas, Stralsund:—'Here lies Major Malcolm Sinclair, a good and faithful subject of the kingdom of Sweden, born in 1691, son of the most worthy Major-General Sinclair and Madame de Hamilton. The events of his life were very singlar and remarkable. He was prisoner of war in Siberia from the year 1709 to 1722. Being charged with a commission to execute some affairs of state, he was, on the 17th of

June, 1739, in an execrable manner, assassinated near Naumbourg, in Silesia. Reader drop some tears upon this tomb, and consider with thyself how incomprehensible are the destinies of poor mortals.' "

In Pitcairn's "Criminal Trials" a series of despatches by George, the fifth carl, to the government, are fully printed, the first dated 26th August, 1614, when he was suppressing the Stuart family of Orkney. They indicate, by his description of the taking of Kirkwall Castle, that he was a professional soldier, trained in Sweden when young. As that book is scarce and expensive, the letters form part of the appendix within. Earl George wrote readily, as can be gathered also from the "History of Sutherland" by his personal enemy Sir Robert Gordon. The earl, p. 331, writes in 1616 to Huntly that Gordon and Mackay, to destroy his house by treason, were slandering him with burning Sandside corn, as in 1612 about Smith the coiner. In 1621 he wrote the privy council, p. 371, that he had no part in Lyndsay's slaughter; the reason of not coming to Edinburgh on summons, his fear of imprisonment by creditors. When Sir Robert obtained king's commission in 1623 to seize him, the earl sent him message that he could be accused of nothing except civil liabilities; that all crimes laid to his charge were mere calumnies; and that he was the first nobleman proclaimed rebel or traitor for debt, without any criminal cause proved judicially against him. Since his succession in 1583, he had been intent on recovering the diocese's justiciary, regality, and perhaps coinage, reduced by his aged predecessor's underholders, Earl Keith, Lord Oliphant, and Lord Sutherland. He bought them out of Caithness proper, but latterly Lord Sutherland, Mackay afterwards Lord Reay, and Lord Forbes, through the last getting Dunbeath's lands by death-bed will, ruined Earl George, called The Wicked only by his foes. Gunns responsible wholly for Sandside arson were the instruments used, King Jamie's court on the side of the spoilers.

Reverting to chapter iv., Hay's "Genealogy," p. 97, "I leave to the coroner a horse," proves the massacre after 1456.

CHAPTER IX.

PEDIGREES, CASTLES, AND THE CAITHNESS ESTATE.

"GEORGE, the fifth earl, was married to Lady Jean Gordon, daughter of the Earl of Huntly, by whom he had William, Lord Berriedale, and "Mr." [Hon.] Francis Sinclair, who married Lord Maxwell's daughter. Earl George had also, by her, two daughters, Lady Isabel married to the Earl of Crawford, and Lady Elizabeth to [Donald the first] Lord Reay. He had two illegitimate sons, namely, Francis Sinclair of Stirkoke by Barbara Mearns, and by a woman called Jenny Byre he had Colonel John, slain in Germany [in 1632], and an illegitimate daughter, who was married to the laird of Dunn. William, Lord Berridale, married a daughter of Lord Sinclair of Ravensheugh [Fifeshire], by whom he had John, Master of Caithness. John married Lady Jean Mackenzie, daughter to Colin, Earl of Seaforth, by whom he had George Sinclair, who succeeded his great-grandfather as sixth Earl of Caithness of the surname.

"When [his immediate predecessor] George, the fifth earl, had built and furnished Castle Sinclair, he went to reside there ; and it is probable that he and his son William, Lord Berridale, who lived in Wick and had a house there, the remains of which were lately standing, as also his grandson John, the Master of Caithness, all continued loyal subjects during the whole of the

reigns of James VI., Charles I., and the subsequent troubles.
For it is certain that Oliver Cromwell in his protectorate
[1653-8] had converted this elegant castle into a barrack, and
kept a strong garrison there to overawe the county of Caithness, which he considered as ill-disposed towards him and his
government. It is also probable that the house was much
abused and dilapidated during the time it was used for the
above purpose ; because it does not appear that any of the
family of Caithness took up their residence there again, even
though the restoration of Charles II. [in 1660] had put them
into the undisturbed possession of their estates and honours. In
confirmation of this, George, the sixth earl, on the death of his
great-grandfather [1643] fixed his residence at Thurso Castle,
the present seat of the Right Honourable Sir John Sinclair,
Baronet. It is natural to suppose that during those trouble-
some times the affairs of the family of Caithness had fallen into
great confusion, more especially as there were three families at
one and the same time living on the estate. These were the
old earl's family, his son William, Lord Berriedale's, and that
of his grandson, John, Master of Caithness, all of whom had
separate establishments.

"George, the sixth earl, succeeded to the title in 1643,
married on 22nd September, 1657, Lady Mary Campbell,
daughter of the Marquis of Argyle, and set up house at Thurso
Castle ; but so reduced and straitened was he in his circumstances, that it has been said he could not procure to the value
of one bottle of wine on his credit either in the town of Wick
or of Thurso. Being a weak sort of man, and very unfit for

H

extricating his affairs out of the total confusion into which they had fallen, and the countess having represented their very distressed situation to her relative, John Campbell, Lord Glenorchy, he took a journey to Caithness to try if any method could be devised of relieving them from their embarrassments. On his arrival, he found the earl so sunk in debt, and his affairs in such inextricable disorder, that he saw that nothing better could be done than expose the estate to sale, and thus perhaps secure something for his relative and her husband out of the general wreck of their once opulent fortune. Glenorchy, well aware of the clannish disposition of the gentlemen of the county, first offered the estate to every man of the surname of Sinclair in Scotland, who could be supposed equal to such a purpose, and who would become bound to pay the debts, and grant the earl and countess a decent and adequate provision during their lives. This offer was made, among others, to Sir Robert Sinclair of Longformacus, Berwickshire ; but neither he nor any other person would accept on those terms.

" In that condition of affairs, Campbell, anxious to relieve his relative and her husband, resolved to take the estate to himself with all its burdens, although generally considered a losing bargain, by paying off the debts, and allowing them a comfortable provision during their joint lives. Accordingly, a general disposition of the estate, honours, and heritable jurisdictions, such as sheriff, provost of Wick, etc., etc., was made out in favour of Lord Glenorchy. As he generally resided at his castle of Taymouth in Perthshire, he appointed Sir William Dunbar to be his sheriff-depute and sole commissioner for the management of all his concerns for the county of Caithness. But although this gentleman was a man of very superior abilities, conciliating disposition, and regularly bred to legal business, and used his utmost efforts to reconcile the gentlemen of the county to their new superior, yet such was the disgust and umbrage conceived by the whole clan Sinclair at falling under the jurisdiction of a Campbell and a stranger, that Lord Glenorchy, later, Lord Breadalbane, with his commissioner, after several years' trial, found it impossible to have himself acknowledged as the superior of the county, or even to recover the rents of his estate." ·

In his " Tour through Scotland, 1760," Bishop Pococke says, " I went to see the castles of Girnigoe and Sinclair, the first situated on a rock over the sea, and separated from the land by a deep fosse, over which there was a drawbridge. The other is close to it, built for an elder son. In both of them are several apartments, and beyond the first are several little courts on the rocks. Castle Sinclair was built in the time of Charles the Second [1660-85], and the king's arms are upon it. The Sinclair who built it was the last earl of that branch." The Kennedy MS. makes George, the fifth earl, not George, the sixth, as here, the builder of this new portion, the latter being certainly the last of his particular line, and living in Charles the Second's time. It is possible that he thus crippled his means, so as to fall into Glenorchy's unscrupulous and selfish hands. The royal arms over the door must show the builder to have been a royalist, and perhaps explains the Cromwellian dilapidation of the place. In the ' Duke of Lauderdale MSS.' of the British Museum a letter by George, the sixth earl, fully explains the effect of the civil wars on his mansions, " I can give account of £200,000 Scots of loss I sustained by Generals Middleton and Morgan (who immediately followed Middleton here to Caithness), besides the burning of my houses, which put me in such a condition that I had not a place to settle myself in till I laid out a thousand pounds to repair the house I live in." He wrote from Thurso Castle, 25th August, 1661. Middleton was for Charles II., and Morgan for Cromwell, 1654. But see "The First Contest for the Earldom," where there is ample information not only as to these castles but about the whole invasion of the Caithness estate by John Campbell of Glenorchy, Argyleshire.

From a minute book of Caithness sasines in the Register House, Edinburgh, beginning 26th April, 1675, important new facts are obtained thus :—" Wick, 12th June, 1676 : Renunciation by Dame Mary Campbell, Countess of Caithness, in favour of John Campbell of Glenorchy ; presented to the court there by William Campbell, public-notary, and registered on leaves 20, 21, 22 and 23." Again, " Wick, 20th June, 1676 : Renunciation by Laurence Calder of Achlibster, in favour of Glenorchy, of the halfpenny land in Strath of Bilbster, Scorriclett, and Achlibster, presented by William Campbell, notary." Those Campbells were very busy in the county for nearly twenty years before the crisis of Altimarlach arrived in 1680, when Glenorchy had assumed the title of Earl of Caithness, signing public documents CAITHNESS. An Edinburgh action was led 22nd July, 1687, by Breadalbane against Dunbeath, Sir William Dunbar, etc., for poinding mares and cows. His son produced at Thurso market-cross receipts that they were his, but would not swear they were not his father the debtor's, and a messenger auctioned them at low prices, hence spuilzie. The lords found the business "suspect on both sides." Campbell's affairs were then "perplexed." Sir James Stamfield adjudicated him in 1682 for £4,500, on which in March, 1707, William Innes, W.S., claimed his estates, only saved through an allowance by the lords of session beyond redemption time till 5th June. The Black Book of Taymouth shows the Campbells at too low ebb to help Earl George, a diligent statesman, weak solely from impecuniosity. In 1648 Dame Elizabeth Sinclair, relict of the seventh laird, comprised for £40,000, her yearly £2,602 13s. 4d., Scots ; Sir Charles Erskine charged for £20,000 ; Roger Mowat, £20,000 ; John Short, £8,000. Spoil, not benevolence, attracted Glenorchy north ; his marriage to the earl's widow on 7th March, 1678, policy.

CHAPTER X.

BATTLE OF ALTIMARLACH.

"John Campbell, 'Earl of Caithness,' was under the necessity of applying to the Privy Council of Scotland for military assistance for putting him into possession of his rights in Caithness. The government, instead of issuing orders or sending any military force for the above purpose, granted full powers to him to raise his own clan and friends, to march with them into Caithness, and to put himself into possession *vi et armis* of all he could claim or had a right to in that county. Accordingly his lordship having collected 500 well-armed men, set out at their head from Taymouth Castle, Perthshire, to Caithness. It would appear that although the Sinclairs must have been well aware of what was going on, yet so ill-concerted were their measures, or so confident were they of their own numbers and power of resistance, that they had taken no previous steps to ward off the storm coming against them. They had not their people properly trained or officered, nor did they meet the *balloch* men, as they were called, at their entry into the county. At the very narrow and difficult pass of the Ord, they might, with ordinary generalship, have defeated a much superior force than what their invaders consisted of. The Campbells marched quietly and unmolested into the county.

Their opponents being assured of their arrival, and having received the further information that they were proceeding towards Wick, orders were issued for the Caithnessmen to collect and march to meet the enemy. Having assembled hastily and early in the morning [13th July, 1680] at Castle Sinclair, they very imprudently marched into the neighbouring town of Wick, where they halted during the greater part of the forenoon, till they could obtain sure knowledge of the enemy's motions. It is said that during this interval they were allowed not only to recruit their spirits, but also to jumble their understandings with large potations of whisky. Intelligence having come in that Glenorchy and his men were coming down the north side of the river towards Wick, the Caithnessmen marched hurriedly out of the town to meet them.

"The only man who appears to have known anything of discipline or to have seen any real service was Major Sinclair of Thura, who had served abroad in the wars of Gustavus Adolphus in Germany. He advised deferring the engagement until the ensuing day, when the men would have recovered from the effects of drink and gone fresh and prepared into action. But being a man of small property and perhaps of inferior family, his opinion was overruled. The command devolved on 'Mr.' David Sinclair, brother to the Earl of Caithness, who appears to have been a very rash and inconsiderate man. As he was presumptive heir to the title, Lord Caithness having never had any issue by the countess, he might no doubt feel galled at seeing the estate possessed by a total stranger of a different clan and name.

" About a couple of miles to the westward of the town, and on the north side of the Water of Wick, there is a small rivulet which runs into the said Water. For the last three or four hundred yards of its course before it falls into the river, it has formed a deep and wide gully or ravine, with very steep almost perpendicular clay banks. This gully is known by the name of Altimarlach, that is, The Thieves' Burn; an appellation which, from its gloomy and retired appearance, it is not improbable it might in former times have well merited. Here the two parties met, having the ravine between their lines.

" As the battle was to be decided by the broadsword, the weapon then in most general use, Major Sinclair strongly recommended his countrymen to allow the Campbells to begin crossing the ravine, and to fall upon them when engaged in scrambling up the steep banks. But such was the impetuosity of the Caithnessmen, or so pot-valiant had their halt in Wick rendered them, that they would not hear of this, but instantly began crossing the burn in a tumultuous manner. They thus put themselves into the very situation in which Major Sinclair wished them to have placed their opponents. The consequences of this injudicious management were such as might naturally have been expected. The Caithnessmen, although they fought bravely, were hewn down by the Campbells without mercy, as they came up the opposite bank. At length the affair having turned into a complete rout, many tried to save themselves by swimming across the Water of Wick; but the river being uncommonly deep at that place, most of the fugitives were miserably drowned in the attempt. Even of those who swam few escaped, for their enemies having crossed at a ford a little way below the scene of action, pursued them into the neighbouring moss of Bronzay, where they slaughtered them mercilessly. Pieces of rusty swords and of broken armour have been frequently found since that time by people in the neighbourhood when casting their peats. Hon. David Sinclair, Major Sinclair of Thura, with many other gentlemen, and a great number of inferior note fell in the action.

"When the foundation of the new church of Wick was dug out a few years ago, there was discovered a vast quantity of human bones, which, as they lay in one place, were supposed to be the bones of the people slain in this fight. A great part of them having been strangers from the other parishes of the county, they were buried promiscuously together in a heap, in that part of the churchyard allotted for the burial of strangers and of people not belonging to the parish of Wick.

"So completely was Campbell's authority established by this battle, that he continued for some years thereafter to uplift his rents and exercise his office of sheriff without molestation or opposition. Sensible, however, that this seeming submission was more the effect of fear than attachment, and that the inhabitants of Caithness bore them no good-will, the Campbells determined to sell off the whole estate in parcels to every man who had money to purchase. The principal purchasers were John Sinclair of Ulbster, Sir James Sinclair of Dunbeath, and Sir William Dunbar of Hempriggs. The first was grandfather of the present Sir John Sinclair, Baronet, and, along with a great part of the lands, he purchased also the right to the heritable jurisdictions of sheriff of Caithness and provost of Wick. His son, George of Ulbster, obtained a considerable sum of money from government in compensation when hereditary jurisdictions were abolished in 1747. Sir William Dunbar was great-grandfather of the present Sir Benjamin Dunbar, Baronet. To show the amazing difference which the course of a century has made in the value of landed property, it may suffice to mention that Sir William paid only 100,000 merks Scots for an estate which at this day, in 1814, is let at above £5000 sterling per annum; so that he had it for little more than one year's purchase of the present rental. When the Earl of Breadalbane sold the estate, he reserved to himself a right of residing for the space of six weeks every year in all time coming in the great hall of Ackergill Tower; a privilege which neither his lordship nor any of his successors have ever asserted, and it is not probable they will ever claim it, their connection with Caithness being long since dissolved. Were his present lordship, the Marquis of Breadalbane, to come into Caithness to claim this right, he would now find himself but ill accommodated in this single apartment. It is still, however, kept in pretty good repair, and is in point of size one of the largest and most spacious rooms in the north of Scotland, being 24 feet in length, 24 feet wide, and 36 feet high from the floor to the ceiling, which is a stone arch of very uncommon and curious construction."

The prolonged buckram style of Captain Kennedy's writing, usually in need of modification, fits military narratives very well; and his account of the battle of Altimarlach will always hold its place as particularly engaging.

I

If he is not aware, from records and history, of the exact facts and dates and plots, he gives good general impression of affairs, and sometimes starts entirely new points. For instance, it was not known before that an Hon. David Sinclair was the leader of the Caithnessmen, or that he perhaps was next, and only, brother of George, the seventh and rightful earl, who stripped John Campbell of the stolen title of Caithness in 1681. That David was killed might be enlightening, and might account for the earldom title leaving the family of Colonel Hon. Francis Sinclair of Northfield, these two sons of his dead without issue, and going to the Murkle-Broynach line, John of whom was eighth earl. But Northfield had not a second son. The suggestion then arises that this Hon. or "Mr." David was really the Hon. David Sinclair of Broynach, only brother of Earl John, laird of Murkle. He was certainly in the fight, but as certainly he long survived it. Other circumstances mentioned may preclude him from the more than doubtful distinction of being the inconsiderate leader of a disastrous day. Broynach's burning of Girnigoe Castle, Thurso Castle, and other buildings, while in the possession of Campbell, shows him of usually far more effective temper than his namesake kinsman of similar rank and relationships. But the two Davids are one, with changes of military luck. It is altogether an anomaly if George, the seventh earl, was on the field contending for his just rights, and giving the command to his junior brother Hon. David, unless the one was a professional soldier and the other not. It is on Captain Kennedy's authority that some David's generalship must at present be accepted; and the captain, though manifestly trustworthy as far as possible to him, is not always right in his statements. The subject needs corroboration for final acceptance, if there is nothing inherently improbable in what is said.

Campbell had royal permission to form a force of 700, strengthened by a paid company of the king's troops under General Dalzell, while George Sinclair of Keiss, the rightful Earl of Caithness, could collect only 400 to oppose those Campbells of Argyleshire and Perthshire, with the above unhappy result. See "The First Contest for the Earldom" in the *Northern Ensign*, which has exhaustive details on the various events here touched.

CHAPTER XI.

THE BREADALBANE RIGHTS IN CAITHNESS.

" When Lord Breadalbane sold the Caithness estate in parcels, as mentioned, many of the purchasers entertained a doubt about the validity of the right acquired from George, the sixth Earl of Caithness, which, if it ever came to be called in question, would affect the purchases they were making. He therefore gave them warrandice or surety on his great estate of Lochow, in case their rights should be ever disputed. But as these lands lay at a great distance, this circumstance gave rise to a common saying or bye-word still used in Caithness, ' It is a long cry to Lochow.' It thus happened that, at a later period, the purchasers from Lord Breadalbane ran some risk of being forced to have recourse to this species of guarantee for the money they had paid him for their lands.

" In the year 1719, Alexander Sinclair, then Earl of Caithness, brought an action before the Court of Session for having the whole transactions between the sixth Earl of Caithness and the first Breadalbane reduced and put aside on account of the alleged imbecility of the former. It set forth that Earl George had been much injured and taken advantage of by John Campbell of Glenorchy, the first Earl of Breadalbane, when he transferred the estate to him on his being bound to pay the debts. The action was of long litigation in court, contested hotly, and the Caithness gentlemen became exceedingly anxious about the result. At last, fortunately for them, as well as for the second Lord Breadalbane, Mr. William Budge, their agent, happened to recover the original letter and proposal mentioned as having been sent to Sir Robert Sinclair of Longformacus, offering the Caithness estate to him on the same terms as John Campbell of Glenorchy had concluded for, together with Sir Robert's answer positively rejecting the bargain as highly disadvantageous. The production of those papers instantly turned the scale; and by the final and unanimous decision of the supreme court, the gentlemen of Caithness have ever since remained in the quiet and undisturbed possession of their estates."

Thus ends Captain Kennedy's narrative on its 26th page, folio size; and that two other pages, 27 and 28, are still attached, numbered, while there may have been more blank leaves, suggests that he intended to continue his historic "anecdotes," as he calls the piece, down to his own time of 1814. It is a pity that he has reached no farther than 1724; for he must have known many particulars of Earl Alexander's life, on which he here but enters, the Lord Hemer of popular memory, as well as the story of the dispossessed Broynach family, whose representative James Sinclair is now *de jure* and *de facto* Earl of Caithness by right of blood, though not yet acknowledged by the crown, parliament, and peerage-books. Lord Hemer's unsuccessful legal struggle from 1719 to 1724 to recover the Caithness estate, has been fully described in the *Northern Ensign* by a letter dated Falmouth, June, 1893. Captain Kennedy's views are thin and uninformed; but he had worldly wisdom in favouring accomplished facts, and in accepting those gentlemen of Caithness who were enjoying the spoil of that Campbell robber. Of him Lord Macaulay in his "History of

England," chap. xxi., says, when discussing his cruel connection with the massacre of Glencoe on 13th February, 1692, and his management of £12,000 to £15,000 of state money given to him for the pacification of the Highland chiefs, "In truth the depths of this man's knavery were unfathomable. It is impossible to say which of his treasons were, to borrow the Italian classification, single treasons, and which double treasons." Barbarian pride and ferocity, the deep taint of treachery and corruption, caring for no government and no religion, betraying every party in turn, are further characterisations of him by the brilliant historian.

Bailie Charles Bruce, Wick, has indicated the local popular feeling about John Campbell, Lord Glenorchy, Earl of Caithness (!), Earl of Breadalbane, from a curious basis, thus :—"When George, the sixth earl, was under the power and domination of Glenorchy, that deceitful usurper was greatly contemned by the people of Caithness, and by none was he more cordially hated than by the burghers of Wick. Every species of insult and indignity which they could cast upon him they so detested or upon his servants, they were not slow to use. This treatment Glenorchy keenly felt, and to be revenged on the townspeople for their action towards himself and his retainers, he prompted the Earl of Caithness to petition parliament to have two fairs annually and weekly markets at Staxigoe. The intention was to injure the principal source of the burgh's revenue, a lower scale of petty customs expected to transfer the buying and selling to that village. On 23rd December, 1669, the petition was granted, see "Acta Parliamentorum Scotiae." The cloven hoof of the arch-prompter is seen unmistakably in this transaction, for on the following day there is a petition from the laird of Glenorchy to have two fairs and a weekly market at the church of Kenmore in Breadalbane. There is no account of the fairs or markets at Staxigoe ever having been held, and it is not probable, if they were, that they would be patronised by the Caithness people."

In an appendix of the above state record the petitions are printed in full, the earl's shewing being that "the petitioner is infeft in the lands of Staxigoe as a part of the earldom of Caithness, etc." As a haven for many strangers it needed markets, the petition pleaded. The only thing to prevent the ingenious theory of Campbell's influence, is that several other lairds had similar grants on the same days. But John Campbell, when younger of Glenorchy, had been involved in Caithness affairs as early as 1663. He was on the earl's side then against William Sinclair of Dunbeath, M.P., whom Sir James Sinclair of Murkle had appointed sheriff-depute. On 29th July, 1669, he had a commission to pursue to the death John of Murkle and William of Dunbeath, and had the Earl of Linlithgow's foot-soldiers to help him. He was therefore in that year in close correspondence with the Earl of Caithness. The people knew him many years before Altimarlach battle, for which he nearly lost his head and property. This would have saved his retention of government money, and the massacre of the Macdonalds. He died in 1716 a very old man. See " First Contest for the Earldom," founded on the Duke of Lauderdale MSS. in the British Museum library. At this institution can be seen printed copies of the appeals to the House of Lords by Campbell's son John, second Earl of Breadalbane, Sir James Sinclair of Dunbeath, and John Sinclair of Ulbster, together with those of their opponent Lord Caithness, which closed the legal proceedings of 1719 to 1724, in a way which seems to satisfy Captain Kennedy.

Recurring to chapter V., the arrow incident has colour from the " Regiam Majestatem," folio 170, printed at Edinburgh in 1609. William Keith is mentioned as pursuing William, second Earl of Caithness, on 10th March, 1500, for spuilzie of his goods, *i.e.*, seizing cattle or horses, selling them, the creditor paying himself out of the proceeds. The arrester or poinder, for legal action, needed a decree and the presence of a messenger-at-arms at the sale ; but William may have neglected some such points against his debtor father-in-law, the earl-marshal. A forty days' adjournal of the case was allowed, to try to make up the peace, with what result is not known, unless the revengeful bow is indication.

As to the actual text of the MS., in order to assure confidence that its contents are faithfully reproduced, what obviously necessary corrections have been made, must be here noted. Some indication is also needed of wrong views, which could not be meddled with in the context, except at the risk of doing injustice or showing disrespect to the captain s honest and interesting personality, than which nothing could be farther from the intention. Closely and beautifully written as to caligraphy, the 26 pages have numerous paragraphs, but no other divisions, such as chapters; and the chronological placing of the subjects had in certain parts to be rectified, knowledge of dates rather hazy throughout. He followed Sir Robert Gordon's erroneous numbering of the Sinclair earls; but as this, with the records and histories now available, is accepted fact about which there can be no questioning, the correct order is introduced. William Sinclair, Prince of Orkney and Shetland, the famous baron of Roslin Castle, Duke of Oldenburg and Delmenhorst, was the first Earl of Caithness of the surname, in 1455; and the counting goes on from him accordingly. The statement that 200 and 400 were the numbers respectively of the Gunns and Keiths in the combat of St. Tears' Chapel, has been left unhandled, as a possible truth, though not agreeing with the more usual accounts. There was a mistake of calling Sir Robert Sinclair of Longformacus Thomas. With the elision of set phrases, which are apt to haunt even practised writers, and with other editorial polishing towards present-day requirements, the narrative appears in print almost as written. There has been no tampering with the sympathies of its author, though in several connections his conclusions are not founded on ascertained fact, his means of research manifestly limited. It is to his honour that he has courageously described as well as he could so many incidents. In portions of the history, especially with regard to occurrences at Girnigoe Castle, and those in the neighbourhood of Wick generally, where he passed most of his life, his facts and views are of much importance, as in substantial agreement with the national records of Scotland.

CHAPTER XII.

THE BROYNACH QUESTION.

To shew what may have been lost by Captain Kennedy not continuing down beyond 1724, it is worth noting that he was the contemporary of James Sinclair, Harpsdale's chamberlain at Thrumster House, the grandson of Hon. David Sinclair of Broynach and Janet Ewing. That he knew intimately this now recognised Earl of Caithness goes without saying, as they were both principal persons in the same parish. Another account of the traditions then prevailing about the usurping of the earldom and the dispossession of the Broynachs from their estates, would have been most welcome, even if hostile. The ecclesiastical evidence which is extant in the county, of Broynach's second marriage, was probably altogether unknown in Kennedy's day ; but accusations of illegitimacy and the contrary statements would be most suggestive, from what is known by our time on the best of grounds. He might have added ninety years of history to his narrative, when his knowledge was at its best, much of it immediately personal. Eighty years have passed since he wrote, account of which may be said to be almost too plentiful, the newspaper,. like the steam-hammer, dealing with large and small things equally. It could well be wished that the captain had filled in the darker period before journalism began its bountiful work in Caithness. As it happens, the extensive discoveries of Broynach literature enrich not only what had till then been the most barren tract of the county's history, the eighteenth century, but throws brilliant light on the nineteenth, to the current hour. On the last 170 years, therefore, the story of the disinherited earls will go far towards making substantial final chapters ; and " Caithness events," up to date, may not be a misnomer.

The proof of the legitimacy of the Sinclairs of Broynach, with their consequent rights as the senior line of their surname and head of the blood, is now complete. That they were the rightful Earls of Caithness since the death of Earl Alexander in 1765, was the cherished belief and secret within the family. William Sinclair of Ratter's iniquitous but successful struggle against James Sinclair in Reiss, which ended in 1772, put many facts permanently on record. When James, who was the grandson of the first Broynach, and who was habitually entitled Earl of Caithness in legal and other documents during the seven years' contest, returned from Calcutta in 1786, with a fortune acquired in the golden days of the rule of Warren Hastings, he renewed the battle with John Sinclair of Ratter, the second usurping earl. Two prints and one MS. have survived of this endeavour to reassert the lawfulness of his lineage, and they contain knowledge amply sufficient for the purpose. Captain James, for he was a military officer in the service of the East India Company, unfortunately with respect to the rehabilitation of his family, died on 11th January, 1788, in Whitcombe Street, Pall Mall, London, at the age of 44,

K

during the proceedings which he had set on foot before the Court of Session. The new evidence, including extracts from Caithness presbytery and Olrig kirk-session, proving the marriage of Broynach and Janet Ewing, his grand-parents, for want of which proof he had been stripped by the House of Lords of his ancestral title, went into total abeyance; his next of male kin, James the Thrumster chamberlain, knowing nothing of his important discoveries, the legal processes nipped almost in the very beginning, at all events early enough to prevent either publicity or intelligence privately to relatives. By his countess, Catherine, born 1747, daughter of Catherine Tulloch and the tacksman then of Brims, John Rosie, he had no issue; and vindication of justice for the Broynach line ceased. John of Ratter, however, shot himself in London on 8th April, 1789, from motives of love, poverty, and perhaps shame at wrongly holding the title of Earl of Caithness. An interregnum followed this last male of his branch till 4th March, 1793, when Sir James Sinclair of Mey secured the peerage without a shadow of right, on the imperfect and unopposed evidence before the House of Lords of chiefly two very old men, Sir William Dunbar of Hempriggs, and a Mr Sinclair, thought to have been Harpsdale, provost of Wick, for whom the true Earl of Caithness was acting as chamberlain at Thrumster House. Mey's printed case asserting his claim survives, as well as other matter, showing the timidity with which he entered on his conscious usurpation of James the chamberlain's rights, who was still under the cloud of ascribed illegitimacy since the House of Lords' uninstructed and therefore on their part quite innocent decision of 1772. The Mey line from 1793 held the title till 1889, when it was further wrongly assumed by their cadets the Durrans. There have been two Ratter and four Mey lairds, with the Aberdeen bank-agent and his son the American farmer of the Durran branch, in the false position. But their eight of number and the length of occupancy have no force against the restoration of the senior and lawful Broynach Sinclairs. Peerage lawyers are unanimous that a dignity cannot pass from the untainted blood, however long the heirs may be dispossessed or unacknowledged, were it a thousand years ; unlike land, which prescription or statutes of limitation may lose for ever to the proper owner after a certain time, formerly forty years but now a reduced period.

Fresh revelation of the facts discovered by Captain James Sinclair, H.E.I.C.S., the first Broynach earl, appeared at length in 1889 ; and the question again became the burning, practical, and urgent one which it must be till settled, the knowledge so extensive and unmistakable. That year three important articles were published in the *Highland Monthly* by Mr Kenneth Macdonald, town-clerk of Inverness, a solicitor. He was entirely unprejudiced, being a stranger, and gave it as his mature opinion, grounded on research in the Advocates' Library, Edinburgh, that the Broynachs were unrighteously supplanted by the Ratters and their successors. Abundant evidence of the fact of the marriage on which the whole case turned, was found by him in print and manuscript, particularly the accumulation made by Earl James from his arrival in London on 24th June, 1786, from the East Indies, till his death on 11th January, 1788, when the subject went into somnolence. By denying that this marriage of Broynach to Janet Ewing ever occurred, Ratter became Earl of Caithness; and as it happened so long before as June, 1700, their grandson could not prove it, in the first stage of the struggle from 1765 to 1772. On his return, he was told of them as written down "husband" and "wife" in the ecclesiastical minutes of Caithness, of which he took official copy, and with personal testimony in addition, to large extent, it was only a question of time and legal process for him to be reinstated in the title of which he was unjustly deprived, had his death not stopped everything. In the same magazine, November, 1889, the author of "Caithness Events" followed up these articles by one entitled "Fortunes of the Ratters," supporting from discoveries in the British Museum Library and elsewhere the new conclusions. Thereafter he made special and prolonged investigation at Edinburgh among the parish registers of the Register House, and the legal books and MSS. of the Advocates' Library; examined and copied out the will at Somerset House, the government office, London, of, as it reads, "James Sinclair, Esquire of Broinach," signed at Calcutta immediately before his return to Britain, dated 25th November, 1785, with a codicil of date London, 17th April, 1787; collected and paid for official transcripts of the ecclesiastical evidence in Caithness, before he knew of Earl James's full copies in print at the Advocates' Library, and also had and made state record excerpts from wherever they could be found; consulted London, Glasgow, and Edinburgh lawyers of standing, with the most encouraging result; compiled numerous statements from relatives and other persons at home, in the colonies, and abroad having knowledge and relevant traditions ; and published illustrative discussion of the various points for authentication of the narrative. The bulk of these labours is safely embodied in the columns of the *Northern Ensign,* for the consultation of whom it interests or practically concerns. A series of letters containing records, cases, informations, and all other instruments of proof, went on from 1889 till now in that journal, making up in quantity what would, if published in book form, require at least 700 octavo pages. No question of descent and legality was ever more amply and effectively established ; information growing clearer and more correct with the increase of ascertained facts, as in all research, till the truth is fixed. Examination by experts of the materials now available, must demonstrate without fail the good faith and reality involved in the whole theme. An outline of the history of the Broynach Sinclairs, the representatives of all the honours and traditions of the house of St. Clair in Normandy (Duke Rollo's Norse lineage), Roslin and Nithsdale in Scotland, Oldenburg in Germany, Orkney and Shetland under Denmark and Norway, lastly of Caithness, will be of use to those without facilities or desire to read the extensive matter rescued from comparative oblivion into the light of newspaper day.

Charters show that the title of Earl of Caithness was limited by state enactment to heirs male, which simplifies and solidifies enquiry. In none of the hot contentions which have again and again arisen about the dignity was this ever questioned, but

always admitted as the preliminary, producible documents
precluding every doubt. So fortunate a limitation of persons
keeps successions very distinct and incontestable, compared
with what they would have been had the honour gone sometimes to women and their husbands, as with many earldoms. A
crown charter in the usual Latin, dated 2nd October, 1545,
limited the succession to males; another, 3rd April, 1592, did
likewise; a third, 27th July, 1633, repeated the clause; and in
1661 George the sixth earl expeded a charter to himself and his
male heirs. When the seventh earl died in 1698, his sister
Jean, Lady Mey, who died in 1716, could not secure the title
for herself or her husband; and when Earl Alexander died in
1765, his only child, Dorothy, Countess of Fife, " did not even
pretend to compete for the peerage." Ratter's "information,"
20th June, 1769, written by Henry Dundas, afterwards Viscount Melville, says, " It is an agreed point that the dignity
and honours of Caithness descend to whosoever shall establish
himself to be the lineal heir-male of the family." Earl James's
counsel George Ogilvie in the opposing "information," 22nd
June, 1769, says, "The honours of Caithness go to the heir-
male." Henry Erskine, the famous Lord-Advocate, in his case
for Earl James, 25th July, 1787, said, " The honours of Caithness are descendible to the heir-male of the family ;" and Alexander Abercromby for John of Ratter in the case 28th July,
1787, begins with the words, "The title and dignity of Earl of
Caithness are limited to heirs-male." On this essential there is
therefore complete unanimity.

CHAPTER XIII.

BROYNACH AND JANET EWING.

THE biography of the Hon. David Sinclair, first of Broynach, and that of his descendants, will now assume the proper importance. David was the only brother of John, eighth Earl of Caithness, laird of Murkle, and the year of his birth has been reckoned to be 1642, that of his death certainly 1714. The mother of the two was Stuart, niece of the Earl of Galloway, and their father's mother of the same royal race ; the latter the grand-daughter of James the Fifth, her mother a Kennedy, Countess of Strathearn and Orkney. His personal attractions gave the sobriquet of " Bochie Davie " or " Bonnie Davie " to the younger brother ; and that Stuart blood in him was not inoperative, is shown by early summonses before the kirk-session and presbytery for discipline, as their minutes still testify. From 4th October, 1671, till 2nd May, 1683, he has frequent appearances in their books for illicit cohabitation and multilapse with Agnes Barny, Olrig. He was not an intractable person is proved by a minute of the presbytery (presided over by the bishop) dated Thurso, 3rd January, 1683, where it is noted that he had given obedience to the then episcopal church discipline. That there has never been a whisper of marriage to this woman, for whom he must have had true affection, judging from the length of the entanglement, illustrates, by contrast of noisy debate, the fact of a real ceremony between him and a later love of his. It would have been easy to pass over this earlier passage in his life, but it is always mistake to hide ascertained fact in cases of the kind, inferences of value coming from the most unlikely sources.

The date of Broynach's marriage to a daughter of William Sinclair of Dunn is not known as yet, but it could not well be before 1683, the Barny attachment continuing at least till then. It is pretty certain that this wife died in 1697, and a witness (Ratter's proof) swears that he knew three of their children, John, James, and Elizabeth. These two males died without issue, by a consensus of depositions; the latter of them, who was the longer liver, in 1754, a bachelor. Elizabeth became Mrs Whyte, Thurso, and reached a great age, of whom much is known, and who remains a principal witness towards the rehabilitation of her father's male descendants by his second wife as earls of the county.

Though his private history as founder of the Broynach family has the leading claim on attention, yet before entering upon its cardinal passage, it may be noted that the Hon. David was hotly engaged in the public doings of his time. Captain Kennedy makes him the leader of the Caithness force at the battle of Altimarlach on 13th July, 1680, with the Argyle and Perth Campbells, who were nearly double their opponents in number and supported by government musketeers. To those who have examined the position of the invaders on a round flat-topped hill or rising ground near the left bank of Wick river, with a huge natural ditch or difficult little ravine, to alternate its description, surrounding a considerable portion of their encampment, the courage of making an open attack on the strangers seems phenomenal, hatred of Lord Glenorchy and his hordes only a partial explanation. In war wonders of panic sometimes occur to justify following heroic impulse, but David was not favoured by fortune in this instance, for all the bravery undoubtedly displayed. He had his revenges in subsequent fights with Campbell's men at Girnigoe Castle, which he unwillingly ruined by artillery, and at other places where they had taken possession. In the end he had the satisfaction of seeing the intruder stripped ignominiously of the Caithness title, which he had filched from the rightful heir George Sinclair of Keiss, thereafter earl till his death in 1698. Broynach's efforts in behalf of his near kinsman at all risks, even declared rebel by the government of Scotland, are recounted in Mackay and other historians' pages, as also in the privy council minutes. He survives well, too, in the popular memory and sympathies; his unavoidable defeat counterbalanced by successes which showed that he was a gallant officer, evidently of technical training, by his besieging and taking castles. That he was, according to Kennedy, general on the unlucky day of Altimar-lach implies professional knowledge. The chief interest in him now, however, is with regard to lineage, to which return must be made.

When David's first wife died in 1697, Broynach House was left without guidance, three children needing woman's care. One of the Colquhoun baronets of Luss, who was patron of

L

some Caithness churches, recommended a trusty domestic of his
at Rossdhu Castle, beside Loch Lomond, as a housekeeper.
She was the daughter of Donald Ewing, laird of Bernice,
Argyleshire, such appointments then frequent in her class.
The mansion-house of the estate is still in good preservation,
a square block with two chimneys, its length 45 feet and
breadth 27, with two windows and a door in front on the lower
story and three windows on the upper, the elevation showing a
great expanse of dead wall, partly because of the smallness of
the windows of the period. Its extent is indicated by its containing 16 rooms, the back having windows on account of its
being a double house. These particulars need mentioning,
because one of the weapons used falsely by the usurpers was
that this woman came of a low rank unworthy of alliance to
a superior family, the implication being that she could not have
a good marriage in her circumstances. But her people to
this day belong to the landed class. Sir Archibald Ewing,
baronet, who died in 1893, aged 75, M.P. many years for
Dumbartonshire, was laird of Ballikinrain, Stirlingshire, and
of Gollanfield, Inverness-shire ; and in a public meeting in
Glasgow he declared that he was descended from the Ewings
of Bernice, his interest in genealogy and antiquities giving
his statement special value. His personalty has been proved
at about £80,000 above £1,000,000 ; his son Sir William,
Ardencaple Castle, succeeding him in the baronetcy. The
house of Caithness has every reason to be proud of its
Ewing relatives, though its enemies did all they knew to
degrade Janet Ewing and her memory for their own selfish

purposes, on the allegation that she was only a common servant of the lowest class.

Not long after her arrival in Caithness, an attachment sprang up between the housekeeper and her master ; but, it is in evidence, more on his side than hers, loyal to her duty and office. Ultimately he gained her affections, and in 1699 the single fault of a brave and womanly life befel her, the birth to him of an illegitimate son. The kirk-session of Olrig were at once engaged about the necessary discipline, which both Broynach and she refused to undergo ; and the serious consequence was that they were summoned to appear before the presbytery at Thurso on 11th November, 1699. As they did not answer to the citation, the minister of Olrig, Rev. William Macbeath, was empowered to "proceed against them in order to excommunication." The dreaded sentence of excommunication by the church usually deprived a man of his property, as well as of other social needs ; and presbyterianism being at its most triumphant period, with the help of the Hon. David's brother Earl John, who violently opposed a proposed marriage between the erring pair, the house and lands of Broynach were, it is believed, then taken away from him. Before the presbytery process, the clergy had gone to Broynach House and turned Janet Ewing out of it, against the will of her master. For some time she lived in a cothouse in Bowermadden, till a culmination came to their affairs. Of date Thurso, December 6th, 1699, the presbytery gave over "David Sinclair of Broynach and Janet Ewing, his concubine," to quote the existing minute, with its harsh ecclesiastical language, "to the sheriff to cause apprehend the said obstinate scandalous persons, in order to be dealt with according to the terms of the act of parliament against prophaneness." The fine for a first fault was by statute of 1st February, 1649, £400 Scots to a nobleman, £200 to a laird, and so on downwards to £10 Scots for an ordinary person, the same scale applicable to women. Imprisonment on bread and water eight days, concluding with two hours in the public stocks, was the alternative of the act of 1567, if money was not paid; but the details of physical punishment varied with the periods, localities, and demands of the clergy upon the civil arm. Multilapse had its correspondent severity of retribution as marked out in the acts, banishment from the town or parish forever the last resort of the law. It is easy to realise Broynach's difficulties, because presbyterianism since the revolution of 1688 was at its utmost of strictness and power, the landed class under its authority as much as the poorest. Whether Janet Ewing was not allowed to escape on a fine, or that, at a time of distress when rents were unpaid, Broynach was unable to meet it, she was forcibly carried off to Thurso " to underlie the law," as the phrase went. It is possible that excommunication had made him impecunious, suddenly; though the whole Murkle family, of which he was the second person, were in impoverishment from the annexation of the earldom estate by the Earl of Breadalbane. How his feelings were outraged can be understood from the fact that, on the morning of the day appointed for Janet Ewing to be drummed through the streets of Thurso, with a paper crown having the inscription of her single offence, he went to the official who was to finish her punishment by so many lashes on the bare shoulders, and "treated" him, so that he might do his ugly work as gently as possible. A mob led by two clergymen began carrying out the sentence, and the point was reached where the scourging had to take place. Broynach could repress himself no longer, and with a primed pistol and drawn sword he attacked the ribald procession, the ministers the first to flee. He put a plaid around her already stripped back, and conveyed her away with him to his home.

It was in no spirit of defiance of the then omnipotent kirk that he kept her there ; for he entreated the Rev. William Innes, Thurso, their special persecutor, and others of the neighbourhood, to marry them, but without success, as they might so escape a portion of church discipline. The two set out for Orkney to try to get the ceremony performed there, and they had arrived at Scarfskerry to cross the Pentland Firth, when a party of men sent after them by Earl John seized and brought them back. An incident of the sort was not very likely to reconcile a man of Broynach's spirit to the situation, and he came to a speedy decision fraught with such danger as can hardly at all be now appreciated, that they would get married by an "outed" episcopal clergyman. The witnesses to the ceremony had to run the danger of fines and imprisonment, while the disestablished performer subjected himself to banishment to the American plantations, and death if he returned, the married pair further liable to imprisonment and fine. The episcopalians and presbyterians, as they were in power, availed themselves of these laws against people out of the supremacy ; but neither sect could, though they eagerly would, affect in the least the validity of marriages actually celebrated, if even without the proclamation of banns. On one of the first days of June, 1700, the Rev. Arthur Anderson, who had been episcopal minister of Kilmany, Fifeshire, married the Hon. David Sinclair of Broynach and Janet Ewing at Cairnsburn House, in the immediate vicinity of what is now Barrogill Castle, Mey, as he humanely said, " to put them out of the necessity of sinning." Elizabeth Munro (Mrs James Horne), Mey, and " two young lasses " were witnesses to the marriage. John Douglas, mason, Thurso, was said to be also present, but the fear of incurring the statutory fine or imprisonment kept him silent on the subject. In the autumn of 1767 Mrs Horne confessed this information, then with fear and trembling, and added the convincing remark that " Broynach gave the minister a red guinea unchanged for his trouble." Donald Groat, on 22nd June, 1700, swore that he saw the same clergyman marry John Sinclair of Forss to Elizabeth Sinclair in the previous April, and that he had five or six dollars from them, which is a suggestive parallel to the red guinea. On the same date Gilbert Ommand, notary-public, swore that he saw him baptise their son " the other day." She was daughter of a John of Ratter, and was exactly in the same position with Janet Ewing, as having had her son born before marriage, both being second wives. To make the similarity curiously complete, David Macleod at that ecclesiastical court deponed that Broynach's child was baptised by Rev. Arthur Anderson, which is a most enlightening statement, in another important connection, as will be seen later. It was sworn by Thomas Manson in 1769 that his father and mother were at the infair or bridal-feast of Broynach and Janet Ewing, and that it was held in Red Hall, Stanstill, whence they returned "to their own house at Murkle." For performing clerical functions as above, the episcopal clergyman was deposed from the ministry by a Commission of General Assembly united with Caithness Presbytery, which sat at Thurso, the deposition sentence passed on 24th June, 1700. For numerous and exact details the minutes of the process, still extant in the county, are of the highest value to the Broynachs, because they of themselves prove the fact of Janet Ewing's marriage. The Ommand already mentioned, who was town-clerk of Wick and procurator of the church, swore that Anderson "married David Sinclair and Janet Ewing, and that yesterday [21st June, 1700, by the minutes] he declared the same to the deponent, and that if it were to do he would do it again." It was the leading charge upon which he was deposed ; the presbyterians referring to his doings as a "great scandal" to the kirk, in the printed transactions of the General Assembly.

The troubles of the Hon. Mr. and Mrs. Sinclair of Broynach were not over with the final step they had been able successfully but with great danger and difficulty to take. Dread of a second child being born out of wedlock to them had hastened or determined the ceremony. In the first week of February, 1701, their son David saw the light, just eight months after his parents' marriage ; and though he was entirely lawful, the kirk-session of Olrig, with inquisitorial malice rather than ordinary presbyterian officialism, called upon them to submit themselves to the church discipline of standing in church before the congregation prior to his baptism. The session's minute of August 3rd, 1701, states that Broynach was informed upon "for not coming 'to church, and for having a child nearly half a year old without baptism." The minute of 19th September gives his answer to a deputation, namely, that he could not attend the ordinances until his mother, Jean Stuart, Lady Murkle, would give him clothes, and then he would do satisfaction to church discipline. He and, as the record expressly has it, "his wife, Janet Ewing," were summoned to the next meeting, but did not appear, the minute of which again writes down the words "Janet Ewing, his wife." On October 30th, 1701, Janet appeared, and "acknowledged a second relapse with David Sinclair of Broynach before marriage with him, as also that she lived some years in the same house with him before Rev. Arthur Anderson married them, being forced thereunto contrary to her own inclination." After this "confession" she was exhorted and rebuked by the minister, and told she had to begin her public appearances before the congregation the next Sunday. She promptly asked for the child's baptism then and there, but was refused the privilege until, as the record says, "her husband likewise submitted to church discipline." Both declined to stand, and Janet was rebuked for disobedience by the session on 7th December, 1701, but by the minute of 5th February, 1702, she had appeared singly the fifth time then before the congregation, so willing was she to have her second son baptised. There is no more about them in the session record, but from Ratter's proof this boy was christened in 1704, with a sister, the third child, at Claredon Hall, where Lady Murkle lived, by the Rev. William Innes, Thurso. Both the children walked from their parents' house, which was "a short quarter of a mile distant." Though always denominated "of Broynach" in the kirk-session minutes, it is evident that excommunication or Earl John's anger or loss of means had absolutely impoverished him ; for his mother not only supplied him with clothes, but gave him the small home in Claredon which was the poor substitute for the mansion of his estate of Broynach. But thenceforward to his death in 1714 he lived in comparative peace, though the ministers never quite ceased from troubling him. Of his fourth child Donald by Janet Ewing, named after her father and born about 1705, there remains no account of difficulties at baptism ; but Margaret Swanson swore at Durran on 25th May, 1767, that she saw the youngest baptised Janet by Rev. William Innes, and that the child was so far grown up that she could go in and out about the house. This would indicate friction still between Broynach and the clergy, Swanson giving the date of the baptism as 1712. From the "informations" of 1769, where the half-sister of these children Mrs. Whyte gives sworn evidence, it is known that Margaret was the name of Janet Ewing's third child. The eldest son by the oath of Elizabeth Sinclair (Mrs Whyte) died a baby, and it has been seen that he was baptised by the Rev. Arthur Anderson, but, passing away so early, his name has not transpired. Of Broynach's family by Janet Ewing there is therefore a perfect reckoning, according to the order of birth, thus : the eldest son, who was made lawful by the marriage of 1700, but died an infant ;

M

David, lawful at his birth, by all the codes of law, even the
strictest, that of England, though his parents suffered at the
hands of Olrig kirk-session on perhaps imaginary grounds, if
the medical dictum is true that eight months' perfect
children are frequent facts ; Margaret, born about 1703 ;
Donald, so well known in adult life as the Sailor, ancestor of
the present Broynach earl ; and lastly, Janet Sinclair.   A
great question has been for ever settled by this placing of the
members of Broynach's family by Janet Ewing in their proper
sequence on irrefragable evidence.   The question of seniority,
as between David and Donald, in the peerage discussion, has
given a world of trouble.   Reference to the *Northern Ensign*
will show the endless difficulties of coming to a conclusion.
Three-fourth of the letters there contended for David, and the
other fourth for Donald, as the elder.   The discovery that there
was a baptised son older than both reconciled all the contra-
dictions.   It put David as second son (with the satisfactory
consequence that Captain James Sinclair, H.E.I.C.S., his son,
was a true Earl of Caithness), while Donald the Sailor took his
place as third and last son of the family.   Next to the manifold
establishment of Janet Ewing's marriage to Broynach, comes the
fortunate and final decision of the respective seniority and
juniority of her two sons who reached manhood and had
descendants.   The Hon. David Sinclair of Broynach was buried
at the expense of his sister-in-law, Jean Carmichael, the widow
of his only brother Earl John ; wax candles and other things
appropriate to his rank carefully supplied by the countess.

Earl Alexander had succeeded his father Earl John in

1705, and for nine years this nephew was the superior of his uncle David. The antagonism of the father to the Ewing connection seemed to augment in the son, and his lawful first cousins were left to get their living as they best could. Their mother at the death of her husband was taken by her stepson James, of the first family by the daughter of Dun, into his house on a small freehold sowing not more than 2½ bolls, which he had given him by one of these earls, son or father. Both Broynach's families lived in this little cottage, and added to their scanty means by spinning and working among the ordinary neighbours as well as for their highborn relatives. James the stepson stayed much at Westfield House with his first cousin the Hon. Francis Sinclair, a brother of Earl Alexander, and was seldom at home in Murkle. Another brother of the earl, Lord Murkle, judge of the court of session, kept up some interest in them ; and Hon. Archibald, the remaining brother of the family, may have been kind. No male descent was left by these four brothers, and thus it was that ultimately the impoverished cousins and their descendants became by right of blood of first importance. Janet Ewing lived till some year between 1730 and 1738 ; her burial under the seat in the aisle of James Sinclair of Durran, in the church of Olrig, the plainest evidence that she was considered a lady of the county, and lawfully married to the uncle of its contemporary earl. Alexander M'Ghie in 1769 swore it was under the seat of the Hon. Francis Sinclair her husband's nephew that she was buried, and not Durran's as other witnesses instructed ; but, in either case, the inference of her being accepted as the

wife of an earl's brother is the same.   Lady Margaret Primrose,
sister and daughter of the Earls of Rosebery, who married Earl
Alexander in 1738, and to whom she bore only a daughter,
Lady Dorothy Sinclair, the Countess of Fife, deponed in 1769
that she heard Lord Caithness, her own husband, speaking of
Broynach's " second wife" Janet Ewing, and regretting that he
had married a woman beneath him in quality ; that Janet's
stepson with whom she resided, acknowledged his father's
children by his second wife as his lawful brothers and sisters,
when he used to dine with the deponent at Hemer Castle ;
that he told her (Lady Caithness) of a daughter of Janet's in
the neighbourhood, to whom she gave linen and other presents,
at which Lord Caithness expressed his pleasure ; that she had
the same information from the Miss Sinclairs, daughters of
Southdun, Earl Alexander's nieces ; and that the second
marriage was never contradicted by any person she had
conversed with, till Ratter denied it in claiming to be next-of-
kin to her late husband the Earl of Caithness.   How women
should be right on such a question is most natural, but written
records of voluminous and perfectly effective character have put
the subject quite out of the field of controversy.

CHAPTER XIV.

DAVID, EARL JAMES HIS SON, AND DONALD.

THERE could have been no hope whatever that any of Broynach's second family or their descendants would ever succeed to the earldom of Caithness when David and Donald were struggling to make some headway in the plainest spheres of life. Earl Alexander's long tenure from 1705 to 1765 of the title, and his marriage; his three brothers' lives, two of whom were married, who might have sons; James, the half-brother, of Broynach's first family, a bachelor, but free to chose a wife at any time before his death in 1754; dimmed the chances of succession for Janet Ewing's descent almost to nothing. In these circumstances the reason is to be found why Janet Ewing's sons were of so little account to the principal representative. But against every probability all obstacles between them and the dignity vanished, and at the death of Earl Alexander in 1765 David's son James was Earl of Caithness. It is the more surprising because Earl Alexander left numerous illegitimate sons and daughters; but his quarrel with the Countess of Caithness about some of these naturals, his consequent separation from her after the birth of one daughter, and his wife's survival of him, effectually stopped the dearest wish of his being, namely, to have a lawful son to

succeed him.   The bitter disappointment jaundiced him against
his Broynach next-of-kin, and it became the object of his
existence not only to deprive the despised Janet Ewing's
descent of the title, if possible, but also of all his own and his
brother's estates, to which they were the proper heirs.   In the
latter endeavour he entirely succeeded by an entail dated
Hemer, 17th August, 1761, which on his death threw his
patrimony and acquired lands, as well as the lands of his
dead brothers, into the possession of Sir John Sinclair
of Stevenston, Haddingtonshire, whose surname was the sole
tie of infinitely distant relationship.   His own daughter, too,
the Countess of Fife, though she had her father's personalty of
£40,000, lost, by his intrigues with George Sinclair, Lord
Woodhall of the court of session, his favourite of the
Stevenstons, properties destined for her by her Sinclair uncles.
Woodhall was put last in the list of heirs of entail, and Sir
John as his heir succeeded to the lands.   Earl Alexander's
family pride was monstrous.   Of Ratter, who had the position
of a Caithness laird, he wrote that he was " of very remote kin
to him, that he had but a very small estate, that he was a good
deal in debt, that he had no education, and that he never had
been in good company."   Sweden was not too far for the aged
earl to have been searching for a dignified enough male heir;
but he ultimately, to the inscrutable wrong of his immediate
relatives, whom he knew to be lawful, dropped on the
Stevenstons in a generosity of which private malice and despair
of legal offspring were the motives.   While there was no danger
of David or Donald coming to the title and estates, the four

brothers took a general but hardly the right kinship interest in them ; at all events, Earl Alexander kept them at a distance. Donald Watt in the "informations" of 1769 swore that the Hon. Francis Sinclair of Westfield "took care of Donald, one of Broynach's sons by Janet Ewing, in the same way one does a friend," and that Broynach's relatives generally were kind to the other children, "having little of their own, if they had not got it from them." In small things there were many civilities and aids ; but in essential rights there was conspiracy to defraud them, and till now the effects have been disastrously working.

David's biography is wonderfully in detail. He was born in February, 1701, baptised in Claredon Hall about 1705, married to Margaret More, *i.e.*, Mackay, in 1744, the contract 21st October by Thurso parish register (her baptism on October 5th, 1723), and died about 1760. Rev. William Innes at his christening when he was four years old, on application of the water had the startling reproof, "May the devil take you for wetting me ;" and incidents upon incidents are preserved of his chequered and unhappy life, especially in Ratter's proof. His noble cousins first put him on board a ship to become a sailor. If he were drowned they would not perhaps much regret the accident, but from that chance he escaped by promptly returning to Murkle. He next took to kelp-burning in Strathnaver, where he fell ill of flux or dysentery. Mackay of Clashinach, who was a relative of the Murkle earls, at the direction of Dr. William Sinclair, Thurso, Earl Alexander's physician and kinsman, gave money to David to help him during his illness, and it is to be inferred that the earl repaid it.

David worked afterwards as a day-labourer with Charles Oliphant, a servant of the laird of Ulbster; and he was also man-servant to Rev. James Gilchrist, who was minister of Thurso from 1738 to 1751. The Dutch war began in February, 1743, and ended with the peace of Aix-la-Chapelle on 18th October, 1748, in which the battles of Dettingen and Fontenoy were fought; David a private soldier on the British and Dutch side against the French. He enlisted "with John Milne in Thurso for behoof of a recruiting officer in the Dutch service." When he returned from the Netherlands, he and his wife and their eldest son James went to what was then called the Moray side, being the southern shore of the firth of that name. There they stayed for three years, returning to Thurso, he in a "very bad state of health." Evidence is given that he was supported with his wife and family, consisting of only two sons, James and John, and possibly some daughters, by his cousin the Hon. Francis Sinclair of Westfield and others of the Caithness house. The cost even of his fir coffin, 10 shillings, "such a coffin as is commonly made for the country people," is sworn to with the important additional fact that it was Westfield who paid for it. Of all the Broynachs he perhaps had to drink the bitterest cup of degradation from his birthright rank. His remains lie in Thurso churchyard, his cousin Lord Caithness refusing to allow him to be buried in the Murkle aisle of St. Peter's Church among his noble kin. But time brings its revenges, and his eldest son is now known to have been James, Earl of Caithness, from 1765 to 1788, the gallant Captain Sinclair, H.E.I.C.S.

To what has already been said of this Earl James, whose efforts have been the chief element in the rehabilitation of his lineage, something further must here be given. In 1767 he had a brother John, page 27 of Henderson's "Family History" states, from some unknown but, it may be, good authority. The text of James's will in Somerset House, of dates 1785 and 1787, makes no mention of a brother or sister among the relatives benefited; his maternal aunt Janet More (Mrs. John Paterson), Durran, having £200 sterling, and the grandchildren of his paternal aunt Elizabeth Sinclair, Broynach's daughter by the first wife, best known as Mrs. Whyte, getting also £200 sterling. The conclusion is unavoidable that he was then the last of the children of his father and mother David Sinclair and Margaret More; for it is inconceivable that he would leave nothing to brother or sister if any survived at that time, his kin feeling exceptionally strong by superabundant proofs. Being therefore the end of his branch, the peerage passed from him directly to the eldest son of his uncle Donald. Of the captain's personal history a great deal has survived. It could be told on many a page how he married Catherine Rosie, and made her Countess of Caithness, the contract at Reiss 17th December, 1763, by parish register, she born in 1747 at Brims, on the same authority; how her father had found treasure in a field at Oust, and backed the young pair in fighting their rights before the court of session and parliament; how on 21st August, 1766, at the meeting of the peers of Scotland at Holyrood House to elect a representative peer for the House of Lords, he answered to the title of Earl of Caithness on the calling of the

N

roll, and claimed his place and vote at the election, but was
objected to till he proved his right; how the Right Hon. Henry,
Lord Borthwick, on 1st October, 1767, at an election of two
representative peers, produced a proxy of his signed "James,
Earl of Caithness," and demanded to vote for him, but was not
permitted; how on 21st December, 1768, in Holyrood House at
another election he personally answered to the title of Earl
of Caithness, and, on the Lord Clerk Register objecting officially,
gave in a protest signed CAITHNESS (for all which peerage doings
see Robertson's "Proceedings"); how he attended courts,
commissions for evidence, the court of session, and at last the
House of Lords till his defeat in 1772 by William Sinclair of
Ratter on the one and cardinal point of not being able to prove
Broynach's marriage to Janet Ewing, his grandfather and
grandmother; how he sailed for Calcutta on the Anson in
February of that year a cadet of the East India Company,
distinguished himself in affairs under Warren Hastings, and
returned in June, 1786, with the title of captain, and possessed
of a handsome fortune; how he discovered in Caithness the
ecclesiastical proofs of his grandparents' marriage, and immediately entered on a process of reduction against the second sham
Ratter earl, the opposing printed cases dated, his 25th July, 1787,
and John of Ratter's 28th July, 1787, the captain's containing
the new information, with additions in MS., he also producing
the extracts from the Caithness kirk records; and, lastly, how,
on the eve of winning the contest, which ought never to have
been entered upon, he died on 11th January, 1788, with, as far
as himself was concerned, his labour lost, but now, after a

century's somnolence of the evidence, the restoration to his blood of their undoubted right to the title of Earl of Caithness. Thanks to this brave man, the Broynachs are known to be the head of the house of Sinclair, their cause triumphant by the patient unravelling of an intricate web of injustices, beyond all ordinary conception in their number and variety. A quotation will give his own version of his rights, when he protested thus at Holyrood House : "That his propinquity to the late Earl of Caithness was notorious, he being son and heir of the deceased David Sinclair, who was lawful son and heir of the deceased David Sinclair of Broinach [he used this spelling also in his will], who was the only brother-german of Sir John Sinclair of Murkle, afterwards Earl of Caithness, father to the said Alexander, last Earl of Caithness, lately deceased ; and that he, James Sinclair, is now nearest heir-male of the said Alexander, Earl of Caithness, his father's first cousin, and thereby succeeds to the title and dignity of Earl of Caithness." The results of time and investigation have corroborated every word of this extract from his "written paper" at the election of the Duke of Atholl in room of the deceased William, Earl of Sutherland, in 1766.

Of Donald the Sailor, Janet Ewing's third son, the uncle of Earl James, the last of David's sons, much also is known. In youth he was entertained at Westfield House by his first cousin the Hon. Francis Sinclair, as has been seen ; and, unlike his brother David, he took the advice of his cousins to go to sea. In due course they must have aided him to the ownership of a trading vessel, of which he was himself captain ; and from

Sarclet, near Wick, to Avoch in the Black Isle, Ross-shire, was his principal route, though he trafficked freely on both sides of the Moray Firth with other places, Banff in particular. He found his way to Sarclet from the Thurso side through his half-sister Elizabeth's marriage to James Whyte in Thurso, who was previously in Meikle Clyth. Donald was about twenty-one when they married in 1726, and his brother-in-law's connections with the Wick side no doubt brought him there ; Oags of that coast being similarly conversant with the two districts, and related to the Broynachs. On 25th October, 1736, by Wick parish register, Donald the Sailor contracted with Catherine, daughter of John Sinclair in Thrumster, the marriage taking place on the 30th November following. His daughter Christina was born on 27th March, 1737, but the ecclesiastical temper had grown milder since his grandparents' sufferings, or rather power to invoke the civil magistrate's aid had been taken away from the kirk, and there does not appear to have been any exercise of discipline, the child perfectly lawful, as born within wedlock. Their children have been traced from the registers in the order of birth, Janet next to Christina, Catherine the third, Daniel-Anne the fourth, as if they feared there were to be no sons and his own name would go into oblivion. At last their eldest son came, who is registered thus :—" 1744, May 14th, Donald Sinclair in Sarclet had a child baptized named James, the witnesses John Sutherland, James Hill." This is James the chamberlain, who became Earl of Caithness on the death in 1788 of his first cousin the Indian captain, also Earl James. The register of Wick parish gives the baptisms of others of the large family, Francis, John, Robert, Henry, Elizabeth, and references which authenticate a Donald ; but it is only necessary here to quote the entry of James, the representative of the lineage. Every scrap of record evidence authenticating all these persons has been given in the *Northern Ensign ;* and, with a wealth of notices most unexpected, the steps of pedigree are scientifically established. From Donald the Sailor downwards to the present Earl James, as will be indicated, though not elaborated to the full as in the newspaper letters, there is an absolutely perfect chain of the proper persons, which no discussion can possibly break.

Next to the marriage of Broynach with Janet Ewing, it has been always felt that the point most important to prove, was that this Donald, Sarclet, who traded to Avoch principally, must be veritably their son, the immediate younger brother of David. Consequently no pains have been spared, and an amazing quantity of knowledge is collected and ready for the testing of the keenest intellect, private or professional. Besides records, not only have numerous relatives on the Caithness side of the Moray Firth, but also on its southern, testified to the doings of Captain Donald Sinclair, disinterested strangers adding largely to the evidence about the Sailor, as he was everywhere called. A descendant of his, the Rev. John Sinclair, Kinloch-Rannoch Manse, Perthshire, has of himself established Donald's sonship to Broynach and Janet Ewing. One of the most effective of his numerous evidences is a Gaelic stanza written about his own grandfather, a farmer and distiller near Avoch. It was composed by William Bain Nimmo, a local poet, more than seventy-five years ago, and runs thus :—

> " Seumas Sinclair am Mordun,
>   Ogh coir Dho'ill a Mhairich,
>   Is ierogh Fhir Bhroidhnich,
>   Roimh so an Gall thaobh."

which translated is :—

> " James Sinclair in Moredun,
>   The worthy grandson of Donald the Sailor,
>   And the great-grandson of the laird of Broynach,
>   Who was before now in Caithness."

That this laird is no other than Janet Ewing's husband is settled by the fact that he was the only Sinclair who ever really was called Broynach, in the Scotch laird manner ; and the time needed for the above descent has the same conclusion. Nothing can shake it ; and as James in Moredun Farm was, by existing records, the son of William Sinclair in the same neighbourhood of Avoch, to which Donald traded, William was the son of the Sailor. The evidence is from within the family, and therefore specially valuable in pedigree law. Another example, of the many published in the *Northern Ensign*, identifying Donald the Sailor as the son of Broynach by Janet Ewing, comes from the inscription on a tombstone in Avoch churchyard :—" Marjory Sinclair, daughter of the late Mr. Sinclair of Dun, Caithness-shire, died 24th April, 1814." She was the wife of Mr. Finlayson there, and through her to this day the Finlaysons claim kin to the Moredun or Muirends family as descended from Broynach. Marjory's paternal aunt was Broynach's first wife, and hence the affinity tie. In historical narrative specimens of the character of the inquiries are enough, but legal argument requires the collection of all the facts that have true bearing, in this case unusually numerous and conclusive.

Authentication of Captain Donald Sinclair the Sailor at Sarclet, a village with a harbour, three miles from Wick, has been ample, as might be expected from it being his domicile through his whole adult life till his death in 1768, the register showing he was the only one there of his name. Christina Sinclair (Widow Manson), Sarclet, aged 79, declared on April 29th, 1891, that Donald the Sailor was father of her father's father, and therefore her great-grandfather; that his work was trading up and down the Moray Firth from Sarclet to Avoch; and that he was buried in Thrumster churchyard. She also stated that James the chamberlain at Thrumster House was his eldest son, adding many details about the rest of his sons and daughters. Her nephew, George Sinclair, Thrumster, aged 69, in 1893 stated that his own father John always told him that Donald the Sailor was buried there, as well as James the chamberlain his eldest son, and others of the Broynach descent. George also said that the lineage subject was a constant one within the family, and he gave as an example the habit of a son of James the chamberlain taking him jocularly by the ear when a child saying, " You are a true Broynach." Eight gravestones arranged side by side in a perfect row were shown by George as covering Sinclairs of this line. Elizabeth Sinclair (Mrs. Cormack), Reiss, aged 87, in 1893 said that her father's father was " buried in the chapel of Thrumster," meaning James the chamberlain, who was placed, George says, in his father Donald the Sailor's grave. The "Statistical Account of Scotland" of 1793 mentions that there was a ruined papal building there. It has disappeared ; but burial within its consecrated precincts, implies general knowledge of these Sinclairs being the house of Caithness, and consequent selection of the best place of sepulture. After the decision in favour of Ratter in 1772, they were oppressed by the false insinuation that they were all bastards ; but, though silent to the outside mind, because they had not the proof of Broynach and Janet Ewing's marriage, they never ceased among themselves to cherish the truth of their lawfulness. Mrs. Manson asserted that the constant rule of honour among them was the reference, when actions were to be tested, to them being worthy or not worthy of a Broynach.

On 24th June, 1891, a conjunct paper was composed by David and James Sinclair, great-grandsons of Donald the Sailor, wealthy and intelligent colonists at Geelong, Victoria ; the former born in 1812, the latter in 1815. They stated that Donald was a captain and shipowner descended from the elder lords of Caithness, and that his people were wrongly put out of their inheritance. Their grandfather James the chamberlain was his eldest son, and they gave the names of most of James's brothers and sisters ; Anne, of whom hereafter, among the latter, Daniel-Anne of the registers. A son of David, Peter, Christchurch, New Zealand, wrote on 24th July, 1891, that he often heard his father's eldest brother Alexander, born in 1810, say that his great-grandfather, Donald the Sailor, had a craft of his own, and traded with her round the coast of Caithness and the neighbouring counties ; and, further, that James the chamberlain, Alexander's grandfather, was the right Earl of Caithness, to the knowledge of the usurping Meys. Peter quite remembered his own father David stating many times that Donald the Sailor was his great-grandfather. Mrs. James Sinclair, Chatsworth House, Geelong, wife of one of these brothers, wrote that her brother-in-law, the deceased Alexander, was an authority on the history and traditions of his ancestors, and that she had often heard him say that his paternal great-grandfather was a sea-captain, and owned the vessel of which he was captain. Another brother, George Dunbar Sinclair (1814-1891), Reay, had similar traditions of lost title and estate, with many corroborative details. Wherever a Broynach was, he or she preserved those precious memories.

The learned Tullochs of the county, who are in affinity to the Broynachs through Catherine Rosie, Countess of Caithness, whose mother was Tulloch, have given detailed unmistakable evidence of the truth of the claim to the earldom. John Tulloch in Thrumster signed a statement on 15th July, 1891, his age then 69, full of knowledge from his ancestors, one of whom was factor at Hemer Castle to the Earl Alexander who wronged Janet Ewing's descendants so bitterly and effectually. At Sarclet, he said, it was well known who the Sinclairs were ; for the Tulloch family always maintained "Bochie Davie's" descendants should have been the earls ; his uncle Josiah Tulloch often remarking what a lasting disgrace it was that James the chamberlain died in Sarclet without recognition of his being Earl of Caithness, attributing the fact to the "rascality" of the impostors who held that title. Benjamin Henderson, Hill of Forss, whose mother was one of these Tullochs, and whose evidence is therefore privileged pedigree matter, aged 80, stated on 10th June, 1891, that there was no doubt the Broynachs had the best right to the earldom, and he gave numerous details, even to rhymes, about the contest ending so disastrously to truth and justice in 1772, his mother often handling the coins which Earl James's father-in-law found in a field at Oust, she being governess in John Rosie's house. He mentioned that Lord Hemer proposed that his only lawful child, Lady Dorothy Sinclair, afterwards Countess Fife, should marry James, and so unite interests, but that she refused.

As anything like special pleading has to be avoided in historical narrative, there cannot be more references to the large body of family evidence about Donald the Sailor ; and the interesting corroborative statements of strangers, carefully dated and signed for most part, can only have mention of some of their authors' names, as Alexander Budge, Robert Sutherland, William Clark, William Cormack, Joseph Adamson, William Stewart, Johan McLeod (Mrs. Don), and others having knowledge specially of the Sarclet district ; the newspaper preserving in full everybody's words of integrity and good-will. If legal experts are not satisfied with what identification of Donald the Sailor as third son of Broynach and Janet Ewing is here historically displayed, they are recommended to the *Northern Ensign's* columns for further and, it is believed, incontestably complete satisfaction.

CHAPTER XV.

JAMES THE CHAMBERLAIN AND HIS DESCENDANTS.

On 10th September, 1893, Elizabeth More, aged 90, widow, Sarclet, was visited, and gave excellent information. She pointed out the house, in the straight and only street of the village, where James the chamberlain died. Being asked the name of the chamberlain's father, she repeated again and again that it was Donald, and Donald alone ; and that she knew this from his people, because he was dead before her time. These Sinclairs, she said, were strangers to Sarclet originally, " foreigners," to use her word, as from the Thurso side ; and while in Sarclet they had a great deal to do with Moray, Inverness, and Ross, especially with Avoch, which she pronounced, rightly, Auch. She remembered the chamberlain quite well going daily to his salt-pan at Sarclet Harbour when she was a young girl, and she was in constant acquaintance with his sons and daughters and their children. He had left Thrumster House during the last years of his life.

In trading his salt he followed much the same routes as his father Captain Donald Sinclair, and used to bring back, chiefly from Inverness, cloth and other merchandise to traffic with in Caithness. The Tullochs said that he never would put his foot in the parishes of Olrig, Bower, and Thurso, to do business, because of the sufferings of his people in that quarter, Janet Ewing's in particular. There has been any amount of personal testimony to the facts of his life by living and dead witnesses ; but, as the parish registers contain numerous entries about him, many more than are sufficient to establish him as a link of the chain of descent, it is the less necessary to quote largely. He contracted with Anne Robertson on 27th April, 1764, by whom he had his eldest son Alexander, who was baptized 17th January, 1768, his father's successor as Earl of Caithness. His wife died in 1770, and he married Elizabeth Sinclair in Clyth on 9th February, 1771, by whom he had Francis, born in 1772, who became a lieutenant R.N., dying without issue ; David, born in 1777, who married Catherine Mackay, but had no children ; and lastly, John, baptized 9th January, 1780, who had thirteen sons and daughters, the author of " Caithness Events " his third son's second son, whose efforts in evidence and writing are thus from within the peerage family, and therefore have the greater credentials according to pedigree law. Margaret, Catherine, Christina, were the chamberlain's daughters, Christina of the second marriage. It is with Alexander, however, that the principal interest lies.

Before referring to him, something may be said of the chamberlain's sister Anne, as showing the knowledge which Earl Alexander, Hemer Castle, and his brothers, had of their first cousin Donald the Sailor, and of his children. The only lawful child of this Lord Hemer, as he used to be called, Lady Dorothy Sinclair, Countess of Fife, had Donald's daughter Anne as her companion at Duff House, Banff; and both Earl

Alexander and Lord Murkle his brother left her the then
goodly sums of £50 sterling each ; the latter having brought
her up, as he also did her aunt Elizabeth Sinclair, Mrs. Whyte,
Broynach's daughter by his first wife, educating them in Edinburgh. What could be better proof that Lord Caithness and
his brothers knew perfectly who the Sarclet Sinclairs were ?
That they were not then the next-of-kin for the peerage allowed
them favour though they were descended from Janet Ewing,
whose husband always treated her as a lady by birth, the earl
despising her quality, as daughter of what he would call a
bonnet laird. To the children of Captain Donald Sinclair the
Sailor, the Hon. Francis, who was a specially generous man,
must have been also kind and helpful. He was the chief
support of the tabooed eldest living son of Janet Ewing, David
the day-labourer and soldier, as also of his family, including the
dreaded son James, the proper heir to the earldom after Earl
Alexander's decease. In Ratter's proof there seems to be
evidence that the earl was plotting with James Murray of
Pennyland to get the young James, afterwards Captain,
H.E.I.C.S., and Earl of Caithness, shipped off to the deadly
chances of America, with the gift of £20 sterling, then a large
sum, and a free passage in a Captain Stirling's ship. The
youth knew his rights too well to accept such riddance of him
as favour. If he had gone out of sight for ever, the Sarclets
might have been favoured and had the lands with the title, the
sonless noble brothers apparently less prejudiced against them.
Counsel at Edinburgh in 1769 said publicly that Earl Alexander
destroyed the parish register entry of Broynach and Janet

Ewing's marriage, as Ratter tried to do with the Olrig minutes of kirk-session in his own house, Mr. Oliphant their keeper preventing him. These doings of Earl Alexander were against the common soldier, his first cousin, and the eldest son of this despised relative. It might have been otherwise if it had been the energetic Sarclets who were to succeed; but who can gauge the thoughts of the man? His deeds are clear, with all their evil results, to this hour, among his nearest lawful kin. Of Anne or Daniel-Anne, the companion, who married Alexander Mellis, factor for the Earl and Countess of Fife, much has been found in Banff parish register, and more from a collection of 34,000 documents belonging to the Scotch estates of the Duke of Fife. There can be little doubt that her other four sisters were benefited, as it might be possible, one of them, Elizabeth, having education enough to make her a school-mistress; the brothers also, it is believed, aided after the kinship manner. But these are points of interest rather than of importance.

To return to an unrecognised Earl Alexander, the eldest son of Earl James the chamberlain. He and his eldest son James were the farmers of Torranrevach, in Clyth; both of them continually asserting rights of which they only vaguely knew the particulars, the deprivation of lands being the tradition they cherished even more than the title; time gradually dimming facts, as it must, to the Broynachs themselves, record and learning alone able to recover the lost threads through the many years of the story. By Latheron parish register he was married on 2nd January, 1789, to Elizabeth Sutherland; and his eldest son, the above James, was born in 1790, though unfortunately there does not seem to be in any register the record of his baptism, registration then not compulsory. In the whole range of persons from Broynach to the present earl, this is the only register difficulty ; but the want can be supplied by an abundance of testimonies from living witnesses as to his order of eldest in his father's family. This Earl James was drowned at the shore of Clyth in August, 1845. He is registered as married on 7th December, 1832, to Catherine Sutherland ; and their children's names appear in perfect order, the eldest son James Sutherland Laing Sinclair, late Earl of Caithness, born 27th May, 1838, and who died 3rd March, 1893. Of this the 14th earl, in the true numbering, the marriage to Margaret Grant (a niece of Lieutenant Hugh Grant, 79th regiment), has not been yet searched for in the register, because the event is known to any number of contemporaries, and the fact can at a moment be found owing to the surety of compulsory registration. Nor has the entry of the birth of the eldest son, the present Earl of Caithness, said to be on 14th October, 1866, been verified in the local registrar's books. These are easy matters, on which there is too much everyday knowledge to require record consultation, though this will be duly done when necessary or desirable. The fifteenth earl, like his ancestor Donald, is a sailor ; but, in the deep seas, and in the era of the steamship, his experiences are different. America, Africa, China, Japan, the Mediterranean, there are few places which ships frequent where he has not been. Whether or not Earl James's native ability, ancestral tradition, and luck may compel soon the universal acknowledgment of his blood rights, there can be no doubt that John Sutherland Sinclair, Berriedale Farm, Dakota, U.S.A., as "Earl of Caithness," is a glaring sham and imposture. What will be done remains to be seen. The truth is strong, but shall it conquer? If Earl James fail to do himself justice, or if he should die unmarried, he has many brothers, his immediate next kin, and numerous male collaterals, who henceforth as they may be called upon, will, with sleepless persistency, maintain what contest may be imperative, till the final settlement, according to honour and law and righteousness, of the Caithness now misplaced dignity, is accomplished.

The entail dated Hemer 17th August, 1761, which Earl Alexander made of his lands of Murkle, Broynach, Isauld, Shebster, Westfield, Forsie, Ormlie, Brims, &c., threw them at his death in 1765 into the possession of Sir John Sinclair of Stevenston, Haddingtonshire, who was not a relative; and Sir Robert, the direct male descendant, holds what remains, after sales of large portions by predecessors to pay debts. In 1884 the present baronet's rental from the remnant was £6,690 17s., and this annual income has not been much reduced by the agricultural depression of these ten subsequent years. It is believed that he has no male heir of his own kin, and in that case the destination of the entail, in express clause, gives the lands next to Earl Alexander's "own nearest heirs." It was a main purpose of the earl's entail to keep up the Sinclair surname, and therefore no woman could or can succeed to his real estate. His nearest of male kin is Earl James of that family from whom the properties ought never to have been diverted; yet a special clause having been inserted in the document, that no earl should possess the lands, would transfer them to his immediate younger brother David, Master of Caith·ness, if a successor were now wanted. Time and the run of events may, however, vary persons; but the baronet's rightful and inevitable follower will be some Broynach, Earl Alexander's lawful male kin by no means exhausted. Though late, the justices, real and poetic, would thus have their satisfaction. To let the crown, which already has too much of the earldom family's lands, seize the estate, on the plea of the exhaustion of male heirs to the Stevenstons, would be a calamity. The statute of limitations does not affect the condition of things, if there is no male claimant of the Haddingtonshire family; the estates naturally reverting to the heirs of entail next mentioned as in succession by the 1761 arrangement. The last word on the question must be left to members of the legal profession; though there does not seem to be any room or reason for their interference, except formally without antagonism at the proper moment.

APPENDIX.

I.—LETTERS BY GEORGE, THE FIFTH EARL.

THE sad story of the state executions of Patrick Stuart, Earl of Orkney, and of his young and handsome natural son Robert, for oppressions and rebellions, does not, except indirectly, belong to Caithness annals. Pitcairn in his "Criminal Trials," now a rare book, has a world of details, and there are national and other sources from which a complete account of an extraordinary condition of things could be obtained, if the Orcadian subject had to be elaborated. It is, however, of proper interest to have here despatches connected with it written by a Caithnessman, trained as a soldier in Sweden, tradition says, George Sinclair, the fifth earl of his surname, at a period barren of survivals of the pen as respects the north. They were copied from the originals in the Denmylne collection of MSS. in the Advocates' Library, Edinburgh.

"August 25th, 1614. To Lord Binning. Right honourable, my very good lord,—Please your lordship we arrived at Castle Sinclair on the 22nd instant, where I stayed that night and advertised the Caithnessmen to be ready to follow me to Orkney when I should command them. I embarked with me about 30 of them, and came to Selwik within two miles of Kirkwall upon the 23rd about six afternoon. On the 24th I sent the herald, with notaries, messengers, and witnesses, to make proclamation at Kirkwall, who was presently taken as he entered the town, most injuriously and despitefully abused both in word and deed, the letters taken from him by Robert, and himself with a minister and all others that accompanied him, kept in different houses all that day till the evening; to which they the same day added this also, that to the number of 300 men, with displayed ensign, they sortied out of the town and made provocation to me where I lay upon shipboard. Because the proclamation was thus impeded, I was forced upon the 25th to write divers letters, and send through the country to advertise and command the gentlemen and others to

resort to me ; in whom, for the most part, I did not find that ready willingness
which I expected.   I had to send to Caithness for supply of my own men, who
coming to me on the 26th, and having then assembled about 200 of the country
men, we took land.   At the same time, about ten o'clock, we landed the
battering-piece with its carriage, which by great force of men, and despite some
difficulties through the deepness of the soil, was presently and with all possible
diligence drawn nearly 2 miles towards the town, and the same day about 3
afternoon planted at Weyland, within a quarter of mile of the castle.   We
marched in good order, with colours displayed, and as we approached, the rebels
sortied, boasting that they would fight us though we had been twenty to one,
and having their ordnance in readiness to have played upon us from the castle,
steeple, and tower of the yards, and discharging one or two of the same against
us as soon as we came under their sight.   I commanded the cannoneers to shoot
at the castle, who did their part so well that by the second shot one of the
turrets upon the head of the house was pierced and almost beaten down, to the
great terror of the traitors.   Other three balls being shot one after another, all
hit, but did not hurt much.   In the meantime, the rebels provoking and bragging
us upon the Ball Ley to the number of 120 men, our captains and soldiers went
directly and with good courage towards them, and without any resistance or
hurt compelled them to retreat shamefully.   In this flight about 5 of pressed
poor men of the country abandoned them.   The captains, soldiers, and gentlemen of the country with their men presently followed the rebels at their heels,
entered the town the same night about six o'clock, inclosed them in their holds,
and now possess the town.   That night I lodged about the ordnance, and
guarded it and ourselves with the rest of our men.

" This day we are busy about the landing of the great piece of ordnance,
that we may batter both the castle and the other houses which annoy us and
our men in the town, and thus make our service the shorter.   The rebels are
most obstinate, and maliciously resolved to hold out to the death, though I have
sent ministers and their own friends to instruct, admonish, and threaten them.
There is here neither bread, nor drink, nor other victuals to be had for price,
prayer, or command ; so that I must either seek present relief of some victual
from Caithness, or suffer the soldiers to starve from want.   If the rebels endure
and continue in their obstinacy, as they have vowed to do, there will not be
powder, lead, bullets, nor match to serve for this service ; in which case I see
great dangers, and many more difficulties than could be foreseen.   I entreat
your good lordship to acquaint my lord treasurer and remaining councillors, and
with all care and diligence to provide betimes that money, powder, bullets, and
chiefly some reasonable quantity of victuals, which cannot be had here, may be
sent to be dispensed and sold to the soldiers and others who have need, at a
reasonable price, whereby our great necessities may be supplied with little or no
hurt to his majesty's money.   As things fall out, so shall your lordship be
advertised from time to time.   And now, after the true narration of our

proceedings and present state, I refer the consideration and care of all to your lordship's wisdom, and shall ever rest, your lordship's, ever to be commanded, CAITHNESS. To the right honourable, my very good lord, my Lord of Binning, his majesty's secretary of Scotland."

"To my lord treasurer-depute. My very good lord and cousin,—I have received several of your lordship's most kind letters, and [recognised] your lordship's great care in sending all things necessary for ending this service. I cannot give your lordship due thanks, but I will account your actions ever to proceed from the love that you bear to his majesty, and the love you carry to me as your kinsman, whom your lordship shall ever have power to command so long as I breathe. The form and manner of all that has happened, I have written at great length to my good lord secretary. I have directed the pinnace home, and also the barque that came last ; and I have discharged the captain, officers, and soldiers the last of this instant month. I grant that this service has been expensive to his majesty ; but as to what has been expended, I hope at my coming to make it all up again by munition to the castle of Edinburgh. I expect to bring with me more than 20,000 merks' worth of brass ordnance. As for my pains, hazard, and travail, I will remit them to his most sacred majesty.
"Thus, not troubling your lordship with many words, I end, wishing your lordship ever to esteem me a kinsman, whom your lordship shall have always power to command according to my pith. Taking my leave, I commit your lordship to God, and I shall ever remain, your lordship's cousin, ever ready to be commanded, CAITHNESS. At Kirkwall Castle, the last of September, 1614."

"To my lord secretary. My very special good lord,—In respect of your letter dated from Edinburgh the 5th September, and come into my hands the 14th instant, declaring your lordship's diligence in expeding all necessaries for this service, there is more than need ; for daily I and all who are here with me have hot service with these most bloody and barbarous rebels and traitors. They have killed 4, and the last is William Irvine, an Orkney gentleman, one who I have heard since his death was a rebel and a great friend to the traitor. God is just in his judgments ; for from among us all, standing beside him, he was shot dead, upon the 19th of this month, at 2 o'clock afternoon. A countryman of mine is shot through the arm ; a soldier is shot behind, beneath the back ; and one was slain in the castle. All this was done on the last day's skirmish. There is not a day that I am idle except the Sabbath. My lord, I will assure your lordship that they are most desperate and cruel traitors, and this is a very strong hold, and nothing can do damage to them except cannon.
"Where your lordship has set down in your letter, of his majesty's advice, that I should be sparing to grant pardon to notorious rebels and malefactors, God forgive that I should take upon me to grant pardon to any who have so highly offended his sacred majesty. Than that his majesty were not repaired to

his honour, by all the lives of these bloody traitors who are within this devilish castle, I would rather be buried. Therefore, my lord, I will be plain with your lordship as to a faithful counsellor to his majesty. I find none except of the name of Sinclair in all this land but have been in counsel of the rebellion, or else art and part; for there is a bond subscribed by 700 of the people of the country to Robert Stuart and Patrick Halcro, to die and live with them. The rebellion was devised in Edinburgh Castle last winter, and if God grant the good fortune to get Robert Stuart or Patrick Halcro alive, his majesty will hear of good sport. I have Andrew Martin, whom I intend, when I find opportunity by sea, to send to be examined by your lordship of his majesty's most honourable privy council. I have caused him to subscribe his deposition, upon which your lordship will get matter enough to make him speak Scotch, if he like to blot his master to be the hounder out of his son to do all that he has done.

"I cannot, nor may not, stop the inhabitants of this town from speaking with the traitors, giving them meat and drink, putting them aware of what I am doing, and making daily and nightly advertisement of all they can see or hear. I entreat your lordship to acquaint me immediately as to the council's mind as to what I shall do to them, men and women. I have taken 9 or 10 men of Birsay who were with Robert, and who were plotters with him in this rebellion, and special keepers of the house of Birsay, whom I intend to put to an assize, and, if they shall be convicted, to hang for an example to others. My lord, this service is not like to have so hasty an end as I would. Your lordship knows my commission granted to me is no longer than two months, of which there are five weeks and more outgone; and if it please your lordship of his majesty's privy council to hold me here till it please God that I put a final end to this wicked rebellion, I would have a new commission, with all the privilege needful, until the service be ended. I protest to God I never came, and never shall come, to a country whose people may be compared in falsity to this. I use them both with lenity and fair forms, as the bishop will inform your lordship; but, for all that I can do, they have their secret communion and traffic with the traitors. As for Mr. John Finlayson [the sheriff-depute], there is no remaining here for him, if I were once out of this country; for man, wife, and child hate him to the death. They have intended twice to kill him since his coming here with me, had I not prevented; but now, seeing me take plain part with him, they begin to endure him.

"After beginning this letter I stopped writing to your lordship, hoping always for better news. The barque and post came here on the 22nd or 23rd September, with all permission necessary for the service; and at their arrival I sent to those in the castle that if they would come out and put themselves in his majesty's will simply, I would let them come out. The last of this present month it has pleased God of his mercy to end this service in my hands. The house is mine, Robert is in my hands, and all are come to me except Patrick

Halcro, whom as yet I have not seen. All has gone to his majesty's honour, praised be God. I have 6 slain to me, and many hurt. The soldier I wrote of as hurt is dead. I assure your lordship it is one of the greatest houses in Britain, for I will bring with me to your lordship cannon balls both broken like golf balls upon the castle and cloven in two halves. I could not enter into extremities with the followers of Robert until I was master of the house, for fear of making more ado, seeing the house was so strong ; but now I shall not be slow to punish severely, to make example to others who may play the like. Presently I am going to drink his majesty's good health upon the castle head. Mr. John Finlayson wishes to have the castle in keeping, but I will not give it till I hear from his majesty and your lordship, seeing it has cost his majesty so dear, and I and mine the danger of our lives. I will not give it to him who so beastlily gave it up for four shots of musket. Nevertheless, what your lordship of his majesty's privy council will command me, upon your advertisement, I will follow, and give the house to whom your lordship pleases. I am to hasten the barque and pinnace to your lordship with all diligence ; and I this day, the last of this month, discharge the captain, officers, and soldiers.

"My lord, by your lordship's good care of me, it has pleased his majesty to grant me a remission, and to honour me with that of which I am unworthy in preferring me to be one of his majesty's most honourable privy council. I cannot say but this much, that I shall try to my death to strive with eagerness for loyalty and obedience, and hope in my Saviour to do his majesty better service than this or else to die ; for I protest to God that I crave no greater honour in this earth than that, by my death in his majesty's service, my truth and loyalty may be known at my end. As to your lordship's manifold good will, and the proofs I have ever had of your lordship's favour, unmerited by me, your lordship shall have this assurance of me, that I shall ever be your lordship's, if you shall never speak or do anything about me but as a true and faithful servant to his majesty, and one that shall ever please, so far as lies in me, to be answerable to his majesty's laws. Craving your lordship's pardon that I am so long, I most humbly take my leave, committing your lordship to the care of the Almighty, and I shall ever rest and remain, your lordship's, ever bound to serve your lordship, CAITHNESS. At Kirkwall Castle, the last of September, 1614.

"*P.S.*—What care and what pains and hazard I have been in since coming here, I will remit to others to declare ; but if the matter had not proceeded as it has done, I should have rathered I had been buried here. I assure your lordship that the cannoneer has done his duty in this service."

"To the king. Please your most sacred majesty,—I have taken the boldness to write these lines, since it pleased your most gracious majesty to honour me so far as to make choice of me before many thousands of your subjects, of greater worth and of more valour and wisdom than I, to undergo this service of the Orcades, which, praised be God, is ended now. The last day of September the castle was in my hands, the rebels for the most part taken, to be disposed of at your majesty's pleasure; and all the country was made peaceable. And now I have no more to do here, but I am ready to do other directions, if there be directions and command by your majesty's most honourable council. When I have made an account to them conformable to my employment, I intend, if it will please your majesty, to come to you, to have such honour as to kiss your majesty's most gracious hand, hoping in God to do your majesty more acceptable service than this, whatever your majesty has to do, or else to lose my life; for I protest to God I crave no greater honour in this earth than to die in your majesty's service, that by my end your majesty may know my affection and truth. Most humbly taking my leave, my duty always remembered, I end, committing your majesty to the care of the Almighty. I shall ever remain your majesty's most humble and obedient, devoted servant, to the death, CAITHNESS. Kirkwall Castle, the 1st October, 1614."

"To Lord Binning. My most special good lord,—I received your letter dated Edinburgh the 20th ultimo, and which came into my hands on 4th October. Before the receipt of your letter, I wrote at great length of the whole proceedings here, and of the ending of this service, which God of His mercy has made to come otherwise than any man expected. My lord, were it not that I managed the matter so cannily, and made Patrick Halcro to fail those who were in the castle, it would have been a long siege; for I protest to God the house has never been built but by the consent of the devil. It is one of the strongest holds in Britain, almost without fellow. I see by his majesty's letter directed to your lordship of his intention to Robert Stuart. I thank God I have never said to him but this, and upon this condition he came out, which condition was in this form, if he would come forth and put himself *simpliciter* in his majesty's will to dispose of him at his majesty's pleasure, I should keep and preserve him from every danger of my folks till his majesty's pleasure and will were known. He desired that I would promise upon my honour to preserve him till I brought him to his majesty. That I plainly refused, for I said I could not promise that myself might have access to his majesty without the special license of the lords of his majesty's most honourable council. To conclude, he plainly submitted himself to his majesty's will. But before he did this, Patrick Halcro had left him, and had said flatly to him in the castle that he would give the castle over. This made him come out upon the aforesaid conditions, and not otherwise. As I shall answer to God, Robert Stuart has nothing farther of me, for I spoke with him, and smelt that he would never give over that house, to be tortured and to be compelled to reveal upon his father, to be his ruin. I finding this, desired if he would let Patrick Halcro come out and speak with me, upon that same pledge that was in for him. He flatly refused. I seeing it so, made myself to be well contented with his answer, and said I would go forward with the siege. He passed to the castle, and in his company I put in secret word to Patrick Halcro, to see if in the morning he would come out and speak with me in the kirk, upon pledges, who agreed and came forth to me. After four hours' conference, he and I, hand to hand, I made him yield that he would give the house over and put it into my hands, upon condition I should promise him his life, which I did. Then he wished me to cause a minister to come in and preach to them, while he should use means that the rest should be contented to hear, and so he should make the matter that he should be out of suspicion until the greatest part of them were out of the castle, and as they came out to give them fair countenance. By these means, Patrick Halcro made the house and all those who were there to be in my hands. The proceedings and ceremonies took the most of eight days, which was the occasion that your lordship was so long of getting word, for which I crave your good lordship to have me pardoned; for, praised be God, although the word has been long of coming, it is good when it has come.

"I look that my word and promise given to Patrick Halcro shall not be fulfilled. Before it were, I should rather be in my grave. As to the rest whom I have in my hands, except Robert Stuart, they shall be hanged within two days at the castle gate, with several others of the country men who were ringleaders to Robert, to the example of others. The number that shall hang who were in the castle is twelve. I have sent Robert Stuart and Patrick Halcro to Castle Sinclair, to be safely kept there till I have done all that your lordship has given me commission for. Since the service is done, I have no pleasure in staying here, for the weather is both bad and variable, and so are the people, for he that would rule here requires both wit and manhood, and needs many ears and eyes.

"Whereas your lordship wishes me to conform all my actions to his majesty's mind, I hope in my Saviour never to do, say, or think aught that shall be offensive to his majesty. Before I did willingly anything that were offensive to his majesty, I would rather be buried alive. As to this piece of small service, I think it but a beginning, and if his majesty have any other service of greater importance, I hope either to die or give his majesty a greater proof of my affection and love. Thanking your good lordship for the great care your lordship has had that I should want nothing which should further this service, in my pains I can render your lordship no further than the assurance of continuance of my service, as I shall ever remain your own, CAITHNESS. Kirkwall, 7th October, 1614."

"The articles sent by the Earl of Caithness to the secretary to be resolved by the council. *(Received 10th October, 1614):*—

I. "Please your honourable lordship to resolve and direct what shall be done with the castle, which is now in my custody; whether it shall be repaired or demolished. Though it may be an ornament for the town of Kirkwall, and may be esteemed a place of refuge and security for the whole country in time of foreign invasion, if any should happen to be ; yet since it is neither necessary for any ordinary service of his majesty, nor a house fit for the habitation of his majesty's officers, and may be more easily taken by foreign foes in case they should invade than recovered again from them, I remit it to your lordship's wisdom what shall be done with it.

II. "Please your lordship to give some direction for the government of these people. The present officer, the sheriff-depute, is hated to the death by all sorts of men ; he is of no sufficient qualities for such a place and office ; and by his former evil demeanour is so contemned of the basest, that he will never by all appearance recover credit, authority, and regard here. Besides, if he remain here after me, he will be in danger of his life, and some new broil may arise.

III. "Though there are great spoil and loss of horses, cattle, ships, boats, and now of armour which belonged to his majesty, your lordship will be pleased to give directions what shall be done with what remains, and with what may be recovered from unjust retainers, that his majesty be not defrauded and hurt.

IV. "As for Birsay, which was the place whence the troubles sprung, your lordship may be pleased to consider whether it shall be demolished, or kept with some allowance, and by whom.

V. "The ordnance which is in the castle and yards, in number 8 of brass and 6 of iron, shall be, God willing, transported upon the ships, with all the armour which can be had.

VI. "Robert Stuart and Patrick Halcro shall be kept and brought with myself. CAITHNESS."

For his services Lord Caithness had a yearly pension of 1000 crowns, besides being made one of the privy council of Scotland. He has been accused of heartless deceit with respect to Patrick Halcro, as exhibited in one of the despatches. But it was momentary anger with the man, who plainly had been acting double ; for history notes that Halcro saved his neck, and presumably through the earl's influence, with whom later he was in good friendship. It was James Law, Bishop of Orkney, who had most to do with these, as usual, fated royal Stuarts, Patrick, Earl of Orkney, and " Robert." In a letter to Lord Binning, afterwards Thomas Hamilton, Earl of Haddington, which he received on 15th October, 1614, the bishop says, " Robert Stuart and Patrick Halcro are to be transported this day, 6th October, to you to exhibit. The rest are prisoners in the castle. My Lord Caithness and I, after Robert and Patrick be despatched with young

Mey, and a sufficient number of able men to guard them, are presently going to examine every one, and the next day, God willing, they shall suffer judgment and condign punishment." The clergy were never behind in sparing the rod. He hopes to secure the bond which Robert had had signed by men of Orkney to forcibly restore his father, the earl, and continues characteristically, " Margaret Buchanan, wife to Simon Stuart, and now adulteress to Patrick Halcro, has revealed most to me. Shall I send her ? I shall put her out of this country for adultery. I will come south with Lord Caithness, unless needed in Kirkwall." Young Mey was son of the clerical chancellor of Caithness, and had gained notoriety, before he was fourteen, by shooting dead Bailie McMorran, Edinburgh, at barring-out the head-master of the High School in September, 1595, the second of the line of Mey lairds who falsely became earls. Lord Binning, in a letter to his brother Patrick Hamilton, gives his impressions :—" John Stuart brought from the Earl of Caithness 4 prisoners this morning. They are in the iron-house of the tolbooth, the ' cage.' Lord Caithness with great dexterity has made himself master of the steeple and the house of the yards, Kirkwall. He has no loss, praised be God, but two of his men—one slain and one hurt." Binning's information was then deficient as to the losses, though they were unusually small considering that Robert had 500 men, and the king's commissioner and lieutenant 180 soldiers, with a larger number of Caithnessmen in support from his own county. Sheriff-depute Finlayson took a body of 60 men from Mey to demand Birsay Palace from Robert, which he seized at the beginning of the rising, but he shot at them, and the sheriff returned to Kirkwall, not much of a warrior, as Lord Caithness protests in one of his despatches.

Calderwood's MS. church history in the Advocates' Library says, " Robert Stuart, son natural to the Earl of Orkney, with five of his accomplices, convicted of treasonable taking, keeping, and defending the castle of Kirkwall and the strengths in Orkney, were hanged at the market cross of Edinburgh, and died penitent. The said Robert confessed that his father the earl, who was then warded in the castle of Edinburgh, commanded him to do that which he did, but granted he gave him a countermand before he entered in execution. The gentleman not exceeding 22 years of age, was pitied of the people for his tall stature and comely countenance." The date given to this is 6th January, 1615. On 6th February Earl Patrick Stuart also forfeited his life upon the scaffold there for high treason, that is, attempting to recover his lands, bought cheap and annexed by the crown. Though first cousin of James I., king of Britain, there was no mercy for him, the ferocity of royal Stuarts to their kin chronic. All of them undeniably bastards by the common law, and their lawful descent by canon and civil law also the subject of hot debate, even with Scotch historians and jurists, their uncompromising violence in keeping precarious footing transmitted from age to age in them carelessness of human life the nearest and dearest.

Orkney events, which at this point, from the extant records of those "treason" trials, are extremely rich, must be avoided. It needs, however, to be noticed that the ruling Stuarts and Sinclairs on both sides of the Pentland Firth were closely interknit in relationship, which as often as not caused bitter quarrelling. In 1609, for example, Henry Black, *alias* Douglas, Earl Patrick's chamberlain, and captain of Kirkwall Castle, one of the hanged of 1614, William Davidson, *alias* Licricock, Malcolm and James Mowat in Ethay, and others, were pursued at Edinburgh for the slaughter of Donald Groat of Wares, Walter Groat, and James Steven, all in Duncansbay. The letters of pursuit were purchased by Margaret the widow of Donald Groat, Malcolm Groat his son, John brother to the slain Walter Groat, and Alexander Steven brother's son to James Steven. Lord Orkney and Lord Caithness were hostile for this incident, but becoming reconciled, the diet of justice was deserted. Nor was the rivalry confined to the result of such occurrences, but it is untrue that the Earl of Caithness acted in the Kirkwall affair on other than public grounds.

. His next brother Sir James, the first of the Murkle-Broynach family, was one of the cautioners to the state for the expedition ; and he was married to Lady Elizabeth Stuart, sister of Earl Patrick, first cousins to the reigning king, James VI. of Scotland and I. of England. A postboy with letters, mostly to Caithnessmen, which were passing between Robert and Earl Patrick, then imprisoned in Dumbarton Castle, was seized on 5th July, 1614. Lord Orkney directed in one of them that if Robert his son and Patrick Halcro could not take some of the castles in Orkney they were to "go over quietly to Murkle, and remain there for opportunity," Murkle Castle being the home of his sister and brother-in-law; the latter for a time known as Master of Caithness in the records, the above Sir James Sinclair, whose son Sir James was father of Broynach. Robert's speedy decision to attack castles must have prevented the visit to his aunt.

It seems his father's remark on hearing that he had secured Kirkwall Castle was, "He might have taken a better house, devil stick him." Did he mean Holyrood House, Stuart ambition always of the towering kind? He had again and again been suspected of intending to make Orkney and Shetland his absolute kingdom; one of the final charges against him, that he had ordered ammunition from Norway to become a prince. In 1607 King James I. freed him from twelve or thirteen heads of accusation in a Latin summons of forfeiture, asserting that he was assuming the royal prerogative completely through the islands. But enough of this other of the unfortunate Stuarts.

Lord Caithness left the laird of Ratter, his youngest brother, as depute for him in the offices of justiciary and sheriff of Orkney, with directions to demolish the castle of Kirkwall, according to the warrant of the privy council sent to him. There is a scrap of Sir John Sinclair of Ratter's writing, or instruction, in a petition to that council, of date 17th November, 1614, that "he was a gentleman of small means, having neither lands nor rents in Orkney, and his remaining there under the burden and charge of the offices of justiciary and sheriff would draw him in short time to spend all his rents, to his great hurt and inconvenience, besides neglecting his own affairs and business at home. His desire was, therefore, that he might understand upon what conditions he should remain in that country, and upon whose charges and expense the house should be demolished." He was allowed 100 merks monthly, and directed to put in the expense of razing the castle to the treasury, the items vouched by James Law, Bishop of Orkney. In April, 1615, a Walter Richie had a commission to demolish the castle, who became bankrupt, the labour of destruction was so difficult. Whether Ratter shunned the disagreeable work of destroying a building erected by his ancestor Prince Henry Sinclair, the First, of the Orkneys, is a query that may answer for Richie's presence at Kirkwall, though he might be merely the subordinate of the justiciary acting out the privy council's will.

Henry Sinclair of Borrowston and 100 Caithnessmen armed with swords and muskets, formed part of his brother the earl's army. See the printed "Register of the Privy Council" for the historical points, and also Sir Robert Gordon's "Genealogical History," who, though maliciously spiteful to the Earl of Caithness, tells the facts on pp. 299, 300, 301, adding that Henry of Borrowston and Lybster, Reay, died at the siege, of an apoplexy in the night. Henry left a son John, who went to America, where he has numerous descendants, among whom are the Hon. C. H. St. Clair, mayor of Morgan City, Louisiana, formerly an officer of the U.S. navy, member of the house of representatives of the state of Louisiana; his brother, Major St. Clair; another brother, Dr. F. O. St. Clair, chief of the Consular Bureau of the United States twenty-nine years; and many others holding distinguished public and private position. They trace near kin to the famous revolutionary hero, General Arthur St. Clair, commander-in-chief of the U.S. army, president of Congress in 1787, and governor of the North-Western Territory. The brothers' cousin May, authoress, journalist, and artist, well known to Boston, New York, and Chicago, is the secretary of the De Sancto Claro Society, the president of which is Colonel H. C. St. Clair, and the vice-president, General John W. St. Clair. Dr. W. H. St. Clair, Effingham, Illinois, is great-great-grandson of Washington's comrade General Arthur St. Clair, who was born at Thurso in 1734 or 1736.

There is no more commanding position with regard to Sinclair lineage than the time of this siege of Kirkwall Castle in 1614, all the persons connected with the peerage family subsequently branching out from those engaged about the affairs of Patrick Stuart, Earl of Orkney. If his brother-in-law the brave Sir James Sinclair of Murkle was or was not there, he is very familiar in such incidents as becoming surety that the royal-blooded spendthrift would pay large debts, for which in the end he had to mortgage Orkney and Shetland. His father was Robert, Earl of Orkney and Strathearne, the half-brother of Mary, Queen of Scots, his erring mother Euphemia, daughter of Lord Elphinstone; so that he had good reason to feel sovereign. The three brothers Lord Caithness, Sir James of Murkle, and Sir John of Ratter were ancestors of all the peers, true and false, till 1789; and the Broynach descendants of the second, have vindicated the truth that since 1765 they have been the rightful earls. It is, however, literary rather than historical or genealogical purpose that is the motive to making these military despatches generally familiar, from which the writing faculty is everything but absent. In report VI. of the historical commission MSS., it is said that there exists a letter written by this George, Earl of Caithness, which Sir William Gordon Cumming, baronet of Gordonstown, had; the date 1619, but what the subject is not said. Earl George died February, 1643, aged 78, in Caithness, a man of many, chiefly undeserved, misfortunes. In the same year Sir William Sinclair of Canisby, the "young Mey" of the siege, the earl's first cousin, died also in Caithness, aged 62.

The latest tale of the many from which the earl's reputation has unjustly suffered, is as gratuitous and unpardonable as the "Legend of Girnigoe" in the *Celtic Magazine* of 1883, vol. ix., p. 13. Under the title of "The Cleft Skull," what is surely a fiction has been published in April, 1894, with a lugubrious verisimilitude to truth that forms the least desirable kind of literature. John Gordon, a farmer near Wick, is supposed to have lent money on portions of land to the earl, who asks him to Girnigoe Castle, that he may wickedly secure the bonds. Gordon escapes, and is pursued on horseback by the earl and two followers. There is a game of hide and seek; but at last, on Ackergill sea-sands, the earl comes up to the fugitive in the dusk, and cuts the top of his head quite away with a stroke of his sword. The attendants try to bury, but in the end float, the corpse, and retire. Next day the tide brings back the body, and the earl's decision is to make a handsome funeral to hide the event. Gordon's two brothers are invited, and told of the sudden death of John on his friendly visit to the castle. They are grateful at the wonderful proposal that the Sinclair Aisle, Wick, should be the place of burial, among the earl's own kin. Of all this, the sole poor evidence seems to be a skull now undoubtedly there, the top of which, above the eyebrows, has gone, the cut of the bone

as neat as possible.   Having personally examined it, two things overturn the
tale of the skull ; first, it probably would have been in ashes there, instead of
good preservation, if that of a Gordon slain nearly three centuries ago ; and,
second, the cut is not of a sword but a medical or other saw, which in one
place after leaving the straight goes back to it, with the consequence of
showing a jag where the wrong cutting was.   No swordsman could do this
with a living or dead head.   If there be a tradition or record about a John
Gordon's slaughter, let the sources be mentioned ; but one thing is
absolutely certain, namely, that the skull cannot by any chance fit him.
The historian of the house of Sutherland has prompted with his false tales
yet another version of the same kind ; but to traffic with a distinguished
man's character, whether contemporary or ancient, is dangerous and wicked
work.   To murder, without form of law, was not permissible to earl or
king in Scotland then, but capitally punishable, as students of history are
well aware.   When even fatal accidents happened, there was great trouble
to get remissions.   A remission meant that an incident of killing was a
fight, not murder ; Ingram Sinclair's death being of this kind, the privy
council record indicates.   No farmer was hunted to his death by the
traduced earl in the melodramatic circumstances of the evil tale of scandal.

II.—TWICKENHAM AND REAY.

THE surname of the extinct line of the English Earls of Downe was Pope ;
and Alexander, the London poet, knew, if not the steps of relationship, at
all events, his kinship to them.   The Scotch origin of the Popes is a new
possibility, and some Caithness discoveries go towards its proof, while
creating, in any case, interesting passages connected with one of the
masters in literature.   Several letters appeared in the *Northern Ensign* of
1883 revealing details of curious biographic point.   In the " Life " by
Carruthers, editor of *Inverness Courier*, references are made to the
correspondence between Pope and the Rev. Alexander Pope, minister of
Reay, North of Scotland ; a complete letter written from Twickenham
being given in the appendix.   There is also a letter, in the same work, by
James Campbell, Assistant-Commissary-General at Edinburgh, of date

April, 1854, describing a snuff-box presented to the Reay clergyman by his namesake. Campbell states that the two Popes claimed kin ; and as Campbell was grandson of the Rev. Alexander, by the mother's side, his testimony would be of high legal value, pedigree evidence of this family kind being always specially admitted. An elder brother of the commissary recounted having seen Pope his grandfather showing the presents and letters of the poet.

Confirmation of these circumstances is given by the following extract from a communication to the newspaper already mentioned :—" Nearly fifty years ago, I passed some days with an acquaintance in Caithness, who was well posted up in the traditions of the county, and who, speaking of the Rev. Alexander Pope, said he was a distant relative of the poet. This acquaintance had a copy of Pope's poetry, which he was told was presented to the minister of Reay by the author, on occasion of a visit which the former made to his relative and namesake in England, and on the blank leaf of which was written in the poet's hand a statement to that effect, with his signature adhibited thereto. The acquaintance referred to went abroad many years ago, and no doubt carried the volume with him."

Another letter dated Wick, 14th April, 1883, has further information by James Grant Duncan, " The Rev. Alexander Pope of Reay was a notable man in his day, and no mean antiquarian, at a time when few ministers or men took much interest in antiquarian research. We are told that our Caithness parson rode all the way from Reay to Twickenham, to visit his celebrated namesake Pope the poet. The latter ought to have been proud of such a visit, and doubtless was, for we learn that he presented the parson with a handsome copy of his works. His presentations, however, seem to have extended to other works as well ; for I have before me two old volumes containing the following inscription, '*Ex dono Alexandri Pope, armigeri, Twickenham, Julii 6to, 1732.*' ('From the gift of Alexander Pope, esquire or armsbearer, Twickenham, the sixth of July, 1732'), written in a fine clear hand. The work is a translation of the Abbot de Vertot's ' History of the Roman Republic,' published 1723 ; and coming from the hands of Alexander the Great to those of Alexander the

R

Less, was doubtless highly prized, as well on that account as for its intrinsic merits." It may be remarked that the poet's caligraphy, judging from his MSS., could not be called a fine clear hand, but he may have done his best style in inscribing Vertot's popular work. If it is the holograph of the clergyman, who was a Latin translator of note, the biographic value of the two volumes is not lessened. As the catalogue of the library of the British Museum shows, by its numerous examples of the Frenchman's history, no better presentation could be made of a contemporary book.

But this does not exhaust the survivals of friendship between the two Alexanders. Of date 10th May, 1883, Langley Park, Wick, W. Reid wrote, " I happen to be the possessor of the subscription copy of the five volume quarto translation of the ' Odyssey,' and in one of the volumes I read, in the author's own holograph, the following :—' Twickenham, July 6th, 1732. Gift. Alexander Pope, Esquire, Poet-Laureate of England, to Alexander Pope, Doctor of Humanity, at Dornoch.' In two of the other volumes, in the author's handwriting also, is this, ' *Ex dono Alexandri Pope, armigeri, Julii 6to, 1732, Twickenham ;*' ('From the gift of Alexander Pope, armorials-bearer, on the sixth of July, 1732.') These volumes, I am glad to say, are in perfect condition, as fresh-looking as when they came from the printer 158 years ago. They are printed on stout hand-made cream-laid paper, with large margin, for Bernard Lintot, of the city of London, who had a guarantee from George Rex (George the First) that no one else could publish the work in any shape for fourteen years. I had the curiosity to count the number of subscribers, who are given, with all their titles, in one of the volumes, beginning with the king, the prince, and princess, followed by a host of dukes, earls, lords, honourables, and right honourables, sirs, esquires, counts, countesses, and duchesses, the total number of copies subscribed for being 836, many subscribers taking two, three, and up to ten sets."

The work was published in 1725, so that it was seven years out when received at Twickenham by the Rev. Alexander Pope, the antiquarian. In Hew Scott's monumental work " Fasti Ecc. Scot.," it is said that he was a visitor to Twickenham, London, " from Caithness," in 1732, bringing back a subscription copy of the five volume quarto translation of the " Odyssey."

The poet's inscription rather shows that it was from Dornoch, the county town of Sutherlandshire, that he set out on his pony to visit his famous relative, and not from the more remote Reay. It is true that Sutherland and Caithness were one diocese in former times, under the latter denomination, and in this sense Scott may be right. It is also possible that Pope could be in Caithness, as it is now bounded, as a teacher, before he became minister of Reay, though there is no evidence to this. In 1720 a money contribution was given him by the synod as "intending to prosecute the study of divinity," and on 15th April, 1725, he obtained his M.A. from University and King's College, Aberdeen ; his Doctorship of Humanity, to which the poet refers in 1732, coming during these seven years. He was appointed session-clerk and precentor of Dornoch 27th July, 1730 ; and was licensed as a minister by Sutherlandshire presbytery 19th February, 1734. It was not till the 2nd April of this year that he was called to Reay, where he was ordained to the charge on 5th September, the natural inference being that his London visit was from Dornoch. In the second edition of Calder's "History of Caithness," p. 228, there is a note to a quotation from Carruther's memoir which comes to the same conclusion. The extract is—"The northern Alexander Pope entertained a profound admiration for his illustrious namesake of England ; and it is a curious and well-ascertained fact that the simple enthusiastic clergyman, in the summer of 1732, rode on his pony all the way from Caithness to Twickenham, in order to pay the poet a visit. The latter felt his dignity a little touched by the want of the necessary pomp and circumstance with which the minister presumed to approach his domicile ; but after the ice of ceremony had in some degree been broken, and their intellects had come in contact, the poet became interested, and a friendly feeling was established between them. Several interviews took place, and the poet presented his good friend and namesake, the minister of Reay, with a copy of the sub-scription edition of the 'Odyssey' in five volumes quarto." To the year mentioned the note objects thus—"There is an error of date here. Mr. Pope was not minister of Reay in 1732, but was residing at Dornoch, and it must have been from the latter place that he rode to Twickenham." The annotator is himself confused, the date right enough on his own theory of

Dornoch being the starting point, formerly the seat of the bishop and chapter of the diocese of Caithness.

It is hardly possible that the inscription describing him as poet-laureate of England was written by the poet. If it is his holograph, it would be another proof of his skill in fiction, not to call it a worse name. In 1732 Colley Cibber was the laureate, and Eunwins and Tate were his predecessors, after Dryden's death in 1700. One of Pope's friends expressly says that he had no office or emolument whatsoever during his life from the court ; the only favours he received being £200 from George I. of subscription for the "Odyssey" translation, and £100 from the Prince of Wales. He may have been offered the laureateship, no contemporary having the tenth part of his claim to it, and he may have accepted the honour and its income. If he did, of which proof lacks, it was for the shortest time, biographers knowing nothing of it hitherto. It rather seems that this third inscription in the "Odyssey" must have been inserted after the death of Rev. Alexander Pope, Reay ; for he could not be mistaken about whether his relative was poet-laureate. Other facts and dates of this particular inscription may none the less be true, though written by a third hand ; the laureateship an error, so far as yet appears.

In a prefatory memoir to Pope's poetry in Nichol's "British Poets," published in 1856, Gilfillan tells the visit story from Carruthers. He also gives the information that the poet's height was four feet, every one aware of the weakness of his body, which needed the support of stays before he could leave his bed. Though intellectually his Reay kinsman was his inferior, as indeed were all the men of his time, physically he had the most extraordinary contrast of superiority. His bodily strength is a tradition in his parish to this day. "He used," says Carruthers, " to drive his graceless parishioners to church with a stick, when he found them engaged on Sundays at games out of doors." Personal struggles with some of the strongest and fiercest of his flock, invariably ended in conquest by the muscular parson.

But he was everything rather than a mere athlete. His pen in that remote sphere was always at work, shewing his kinship in writing faculty, as well as otherwise, to the little hunchback who ruled the literary kingdom of English in that day. He translated what referred to Caithness from the history in Latin of old Orkney, written by the Norse historiographer Torfæus. In Pennant's "Tour," the Appendix No. V., which gives the statistics and antiquities of Caithness and Sutherland, was written by him ; and much of the information about the same localities in the great traveller Bishop Pococke's "Tours in Scotland, 1747, 1750, 1760," was clearly from his stores, though not acknowledged by the prelate. "The Rev. Murdo Macdonald, Durness, the Rev. Alexander Pope, Reay, and the Rev. Martin Macpherson, Golspie," says the bishop's editor, D. W. Kemp, Edinburgh, "all gave him information, and are never so much as mentioned." Pope tells Pennant that, at the desire of this Bishop of Ossory, Ireland, he measured several brochs, one in the parish of Loth, which the bishop had examined. He also says that men were employed to hew out rocks at Brora for fossils, and that the traveller took a quantity of shells with him from that district, where he also visited a cave which he said was like the caves near Bethlehem. In a book published at London, 1780, "Antiquities and Scenery of the North of Scotland, In a Series of Letters to Thomas Pennant, Esquire, By the Rev. Charles Cordiner, Minister of St. Andrew's Chapel, Banff," there are extracts from Pope of Reay's extracted translations of the "Orcades" of Torfæus, the learned Icelander, which, with Cordiner's introduction and conclusion, make 50 pages. In the letter of 25th June, 1776, to Pennant, he writes, "I rode down to the coast at the church of Reay, and had for several hours the pleasure of Mr Pope's conversation, who has already made himself known to you by his account of the antiquities and other things remarkable in these countries. I received much entertainment from his free communication of whatever further occurred on these subjects, or had reference to the objects of my journey, and I shall, as I pass along, use his observations to correct or enlarge my own." He did utilise fully the generosity of the antiquary, and reveals that Pennant not only had information from Pope but drawings from which some of the engravings in his well-known books were taken. The best literary survival of the poet's relative is to be found in the fifth volume of the "Archæologia," the official proceedings and papers of the Society of Antiquaries of London. Its number is 20, beginning on page 216, and it is entitled, "A Description of the Dun of Dornadilla, by the Rev. Mr. Alexander Pope, minister of

Reay, in a letter to Mr. George Paton of Edinburgh, communicated by Mr. Gough, and read March 14th, 1777." In it he recounts his aid to Mr. Pennant and Mr. Cordiner, and also his giving of a short dissertation on Pictish buildings to Dr. Pococke, Bishop of Ossory, in 1760-1, "when he travelled through this country." Bishop Stillingfleet of Worcester had described the Dun of Dornadilla in the Reay forest 70 or 80 years before Pope's paper.

The eighteenth century was notable for its love of quaint antiquities and monumental history, Sloane, Pococke, Stukeley, Ducarel, Da Costa, Milles, typical names of the time; and the Rev. Alexander Pope well deserves place among them. In Nichol's numerous volumes entitled "Literary Anecdotes" and "Literary Illustrations," a perfect saturnalia of the subjects peculiar to the period are to be found. It is not too much to say that if the remote minister had been situated in or near London, he might have been the greatest among those magnates, who were collectors rather than of original faculty.

As it was, he had the fame of "an able and popular preacher" in his district, and proofs of his energy as an organising ruling pastor are still extant. He began in 1745 the first register of births, deaths, and marriages of Reay parish, now preserved in the Register House, Edinburgh. This was the year of Prince Charles Stuart's attempt to secure the throne, and it is possible that the troubles may have destroyed volumes previous to that date. Of ecclesiastical and civil law Pope knew much, in the most practical ways. In 1736 he began a process before the court of session for stipend, and carried his point; but he did not succeed with another as to a glebe, because the Bishop of Caithness had put special reservations on the church land in 1622. In 1774 he had a decree from the lords of session for a school, and a sum of money also to build a schoolmaster's house, the General Assembly of the Church of Scotland having had to pay the legal expenses of the process. In June, 1740, he had been able to cause the heritors to begin to build a new manse or parsonage; and in 1739 the still existing parish church of Reay was founded, the old St. Colman's Church, situated in the churchyard, now demolished except one aisle or chapel, the burial place of the

Mackays of Bighouse, a branch of the Lord Reay family. The school process is dated by Morrison in his " Decisions of the Court of Session " as begun July 31st, 1773. The moderator of the presbytery of Caithness and Rev. Alexander Pope, Reay, pursued the heritors of Reay, on the ground that there was no parochial school as the statute of 1696 ordained. The heritors contemned the presbytery's summons, and the commissioners of supply of the county refused to convene. The lord ordinary of the court of session ordered the heritors to meet, but only William Innes of Sandside, one of the principal heritors or proprietors, appeared, and he and Pope transmitted a report to the clerk of the process at Edinburgh, with a memorial. The court of session found that 200 merks were a proper salary, and that £20 sterling were necessary to build a schoolhouse on the acre of land given in donation by Mr. Innes of Sandside, the heritors to pay accordingly. This may be enough to show that the clergyman's historical studies by no means encroached on his pastoral duties. He was twice married, and had sons and daughters of distinction, one of the sons being his assistant, but pre-deceasing him, Rev. James Pope, A.M., Aberdeen University. Of the family, Scott in " Fasti Ecc. Scot." gives numerous details. The Rev. Alexander Pope himself died 2nd March, 1782, surviving his relative and namesake the poet 38 years.

The question of their lineage has some further illustration, though not what can be called absolute proof. It will be found suggestive that the Reay antiquary was the son of Rev. Hector Pope, episcopal clergyman of Loth, Sutherlandshire, in connection with the following passage from Sir Robert Gordon's " History of the Earldom of Sutherland to 1630," pp. 256-7-8 :—

" In the days of Earl Alexander " [the historian's father], " about the year 1585, there came into Sutherland one called ' Mr.' William Pope, a reasonably good scholar and of quick and ready wit. This man was first admitted to be schoolmaster in the town of Dornoch ; then he was appointed resident minister in the same place ; and withal came to be chantor of the diocese of Caithness. In process of time, by his virtue and intelligence, he became wealthy and of good account in the Sutherland country. His brothers Charles and Thomas perceiving his good success, came also thither, out of Ross, where they were born, thinking to settle their fortunes with their elder brother. Thomas Pope was made chancellor of the diocese of Caithness and minister at Rogart. Charles Pope was a public-notary and a messenger-at-arms, who, being of an affable and merry conversation, so behaved himself that he procured the love of his master the Earl of Sutherland, and the good liking of all the countrymen, so that in the end he was made sheriff-clerk of Sutherland. These three brothers married in Sutherland, anchoring their fortunes in that country, but as wealth and prosperity beget pride, so pride brings with it a certain contempt of others. These brothers, dwelling for the most part in Dornoch, being provident and wealthy, thought by progress of time to purchase and buy the most part of the tenements of that town, and drive the ancient and natural inhabitants from their possessions. This the townsmen in the end perceiving, they grumbled at heart, though they could take no just exception, seeing that the brothers purchased the same with their money ; but they determined within themselves to show their hatred and revenge when occasion should serve. At last, upon a particular quarrel between one of these brothers and one of the inhabitants of the town, their ruin thus followed. Every man being departed from the town of Dornoch to a convention at Strathully" [where Helmsdale is now situated, the troops also of the Earl of Caithness and of Mackay of Strathnaver there, all treating about peace], "in 1607, except William Murray, a boyer, and some few others, who were also ready to go away next morning, the Rev. William and the Rev. Thomas Pope, with a few of the ministry, had a meeting at Dornoch about some church affairs. After they had dissolved the meeting, they went to breakfast at an inn or victualling-house of the town. As they were at breakfast, John Macphaill" [that is, Mackay] "entered the house, and asked some drink for his money, which the mistress of the house refused to give him, thereby to be rid of his company, because she knew him to be a brawling fellow. John Macphaill taking this refusal in evil part reproved the woman, and spoke somewhat stubbornly to the ministers, who began to excuse her. On this the Rev. Thomas Pope threatened him, and he thrust into Thomas's arm an arrow, with a broad forked head, which he then held in his hand. Being parted at that time, the Rev. William and his brother the Rev. Thomas came the same evening into the churchyard with their swords upon them. John Macphaill perceiving this, and taking it as a provocation, he went with all diligence and acquainted his nephew Hugh Macphaill, and his brother-in-law William Murray the boyer. They being glad to find this occasion to revenge their old grudge against the brothers, hastened forth, and meeting with them in the churchyard fell a quarrelling, and from quarrelling to fighting. Charles Pope had been all that day from home, and on his return, understanding what case his brothers were in, he came with sudden haste to the fatal place of his ruin and end. They fought a little while. In the end Charles hurt William Murray in the face, and thereupon William Murray killed him. The Rev. William and the Rev. Thomas Pope were both severely wounded by John Macphaill and his nephew Hugh Macphaill, and were lying in that place for dead persons without hope of recovery. They recovered afterwards, however, beyond expectation. The offenders escaped because there were none in the town to apprehend them, only such as favoured, the inhabitants being all gone to the assembly at Strathully. John Macphaill and his nephew Hugh ended their days in Holland, but William Murray still lives in this year of 1630, reserved, as it would seem, to a greater judgment. The Rev. William Pope and the Rev. Thomas, his brother, thereupon left the country of Sutherland, and settled themselves in Ross, where Rev. Thomas, now [1630] dwells. The Rev. William died in the town of Nigg, where he was planted minister. Thus did these brothers begin and end in that country, which I have declared at length to show that man in full prosperity should never think too much of himself, nor contemn others upon whom it has not pleased God to bestow such measure of gifts and benefits."

It is more than merely probable that the Rev. Hector Pope, Loth, Sutherlandshire, who lived there about 1700, father of the London poet's double, was one of these Popes. The poet's father came from France to settle in the metropolis as a trader, where he made £10,000, retiring near Windsor; and the constant communication, then and previously, between Scotland and that country, affords scope for the inference that the ancestors of the wit of Twickenham were of North-Scottish origin. It is true that Pope is a name known in various parts of this island, even as far to the south as Devonshire; but these Popes may themselves have come from the north, as so many families have since the accession of the Stuarts to the English crown, the Earls of Downe among the rest. The inquiry is worth investigation by genealogists, historians, and lovers of poetry. A dictionary of biography published at Edinburgh in 1798, states that the poet was descended " of good families on both sides ;" and this was written only 54 years after his death, in the learned Scottish capital. His mother Edith Turner was of a known Yorkshire family, and the Popes were evidently of standing. The Paips (Gordon's spelling) or Papas of the Orkneys and Iceland were the Iona clergy or Culdees, and Macpherson is a Gaelic reminder of the surname Pope. See the introduction of Anderson to the " Orkneyinga Saga," translated by Hjaltalin and Goudie ; where there is also some account of the antiquary's visit in 1758 to the circular chapel of Orphir, 18 feet in diameter, and to the adjacent remains of the palace of the Orkney jarls, taken from Pope's " Translation of Torfaeus," Wick, 1866.

III.—PRINCE HENRY SINCLAIR II.,

THE PRE-COLUMBIAN DISCOVERER OF AMERICA, ONE OF THE ANCESTORS OF THE CAITHNESS FAMILY.

(Read in part at the July Meetings of the Society De Sancto-Claro in Chicago during the Exposition of 1893.)

I.

IT would be painting the lily to go over the ground traversed by Fiske in his chapter of 108 pages, entitled "Pre-Columbian Voyages," which forms so striking a part of his book in two volumes, published in 1892 by Macmillan of New York and London, "The Discovery of America." Handy reference to all the best literature of the subject in various languages, is found in that work; and with an analytic vigour of the most scientific cast, and an intellectual sanity somewhat rare in historical and especially antiquarian fields, he gives the whole weight of his reputation to the view that Columbus only followed successful discovering predecessors. Fiske's treatment of the Norse navigators who visited the American shores, from as early as the ninth century down to their farewell to them about the twelfth, is all that the most exacting or sceptical could desire. Not a word need be said as to the historical character of those events, beyond what he has written, at once so cautiously and so authoritatively. His dealing with Prince Henry Sinclair, the Second, of the Orkney principality, is equally cordial and sympathetic; the Pre-Columbian discoverer of the fourteenth century, after the Norse voyaging had ceased for more than two hundred and fifty years. In a very true sense Henry as a civilised man, in the modern sense of civilisation, was the one and only discoverer of America; historians of the future bound to come to this conclusion by all the canons of criticism. The famous little book by the Venetian noblemen and navigators, the Zenoes, of which there is a translation from Italian among the Hakluyt Society's collection of voyages, and of which there are recent English reprints, has full discussion and complete acceptance. Major's enthusiasm for the genuine character of the narrative, is most carefully weighed, and as soundly admitted to be wholly praiseworthy. In this field of decision also, there is little room for any new hand, the important conclusions having been unmistakably reached. With his Zeno admiral, Prince

Henry first placed really civilised foot on that continent which is now the home and glory of more than fifty millions of the earth's pick of white men and women.

If, however, nothing can be added to the question now practically settled, a fresh path of interest opens, to which Fiske's purpose did not reach. Of the biography of his judiciously admired hero he gives only the faintest outline, but enough for the general plan of his work. It is more than probable, though his studies of English, German, Italian, French, and of Norse authorities in particular, are masterly in their width, that he had not access to materials by which he could fill in the portrait. If he had desired to accumulate biographic matter, a visit to Scotland and England would hardly have much aided, so far as the great libraries are concerned. There would be more hope in Norway, Sweden, and Denmark, of securing facts about the life of one destined to bulk more and more largely to future Americans, as their typical hero primæval. That, by various accidents and studies, knowledge of the man has accumulated in one's hands, emboldened towards the present contribution. But it is not for a moment suggested that, should so distinguished a literary American as Fiske resolve to go into detail about Henry, Earl of Orkney, he could not amass a splendid burden of intelligence; his Scandinavian research promising much biographical fact, unknown to English and Latin survivals since the duke, prince, or earl's time, for he is known by all these titles.

One of the minor difficulties is this alternating of titles, which a few words will explain. Henry was a Scottish subject, the baron of Roslin Castle, so famous to this hour as an ancient fortified home, with its exquisite Gothic chapel, the wonder of Europe. Situated seven miles from Edinburgh, on the steep banks of a stream whose fame of rock and wood and water is world-wide, Roslin is one of the show-places of the Scottish capital, and well known to every traveller; Sir Walter Scott's poems and prose celebrating its history and glories by many a passage. In Henry, the the Scottish and Norse sovereignties overlapped each other, from his holding Roslin and the principality of Orkney and Shetland; which principality implied historic right, from the Scandinavian point of view, to all the western isles of Scotland, as well as to the Faroe Islands, if not to Iceland.

The Scotch kings and nobility, having conquered the Hebrides, which to Bute and Arran in Firth of Clyde were formerly Norwegian, held closest watch over his position and possible pretensions; who, however, seemed to be entirely loyal to his Edinburgh locality and associations, while faithful to the King of Norway, to whom he paid homage in the feudal style, as earl, duke, or prince, for his northern territories. Earl as a dignity had not the same force in Scotland and Scandinavia. The jarl or earl of the latter was higher than the duke as we have him in Britain, who is merely the first noble. Of the equivalent to a Norwegian earl, a Normandy duke is best example, who, though he swore homage to the King of France, was to all intents and purposes an independent prince, wearing a crown, waging war solely at his own will, and doing sovereign acts, with the shadowiest or no reference to his feudal superior. The history of Norway from Harold Fairhair, who became in 872 its first ruler, shows the jarl on all but equal terms with the king, and often becoming the king. As much as possible the Scottish earls, for policy, and perhaps because of natural jealousy of their countryman, obscured Henry's position as a Norse prince, writing him down in the records of Scotland always as *comes*, which was the ordinary Latin for the title of count or earl as held by themselves, who were only nobles. In the position of being between two stools, Prince Henry would accept the description, as keeping down antagonisms to him, from holding a foreign dignity of the kind absolutely next to supreme. It was practically supreme, for he held a regular royal court at Kirkwall, the head town of the Orkneys, famous for its cathedral and its castles or palaces.

His son and successor, William, Jarl or Prince of Orkney, was urged by the Stuart monarchs of Scotland, James the Second and James the Third, finally by the latter on occasion of his marriage in 1470 to Margaret of Denmark, to give up the principality for political peace between Scotland and Scandinavia; its annexation to the former kingdom taking place in 1468, preparatory to that marriage, as a dowry money pledge which, not fulfilled, makes those northern islands still technically Scandinavian territory, on payment of the sum. William, it is true, had compensation for royal acquisition of his island rights, by receiving the earldom of Caithness in 1455, and rich lands in Fifeshire, Dumfriesshire, and other counties, with a state yearly income, at the annexation; but he thus subsided from a sovereign position to that of a Scottish noble, whose lands and influence were afterwards wholly confined within the dominions of the Stuarts as kings of Scotland. The convenience of this to the latter is apparent, as it finished all potential aspirations of re-attaching to Scandinavia its former archipelago empire, which it is now known extended to Vinland or America, and which well down to King Haco's death in 1263 at Kirkwall, occupied all the islands and much of the mainlands of Scotland and Ireland.

Torfaeus, the Scandinavian historian, who told the modern world most about Vinland, born in Iceland in 1636, and who died in 1720, one of the most learned of his period, gives the exact position to Henry, as prince of that archipelago of islands, in the following passage from his work in Latin entitled "Orcades":—"In the year 1398, Henry Sinclair, Jarl of Orkney (being declared the next in rank to the king, by Archbishop Vinold of Nidar and the rest of the bishops and senators, with the other councillors of the Norwegian kingdom), proclaimed, by a long document, that Eric was the true heir and successor to the kingdom of Norway." His precedence as second person in the Norwegian realm, sufficiently authenticates the standing; his sea-kingdom of the islands, in the days when ships were the wealth, making him probably the superior of his nominal sovereign in actual means.

II.

Before noting further biography of Prince Henry, let mention be made of a notable piece published in the United States, December, 1892, entitled "Honours for Seven," by Marie de Sancto Claro, and also an article in the *Boston Transcript* of 12th September, 1892, over the signature Mary Whitney Emerson, Morgan City, Louisiana; both papers the work of the secretary of the De Sancto Claro Society. She brilliantly makes a Pleiades of discoverers of America, namely, the five Norse rovers from the ninth century, Henry Sinclair, Prince of the Norseland Isles, and, lastly, Columbus. What is even more striking, is her very original idea that all those daring adventurers, except Columbus, the Italian, were of the blood royal of Rollo, Duke of Normandy. This Norseman finally established himself in that fairest province of France as sovereign, in 912, by a treaty with

King Charles, who gave him his daughter in marriage to clinch the bargain. Their meeting, backed by armies, took place at St. Clair Castle on the river Epte, the ruins of which still top a conical hill commanding a view of the richest landscape in Gaul, as is testified from actual examination during a long summer day. When so extraordinary a theory was realised, which made Prince Henry the sixth of his relatives who touched at, and resided during intervals in, Vineland or North America, one thought only would come, namely, that the moral courage, as well as the quick insight, belongs especially to woman, and that in genealogical and historical studies she has fresh fields and pastures new to conquer. The point is so startling, but withal probable, that the masculine mind dare not, till after much slow plodding, say a word about it. Should the De Sancto Claro Society establish such a sweeping and marvellous conclusion, by many years' study, that of itself would give reason for its existence. The Norse discoverers, especially the pink of them, Prince Henry, would completely take the wind out of the brave enough sails of Columbus; though detracting nothing from his essentially heroic spirit and labours. Henceforth he, however, would be considered a follower and not a leader; a thought not in any degree novel, because it has been frequently stated that he gained his knowledge of the existence of the American continent during a voyage to Iceland; the statement prevalent long before rivalry with him as the discoverer, true or pretended, had developed. In civilised periods, Prince Henry of the Orkneys preceded him there by more than a century, aided by the keen Italian intellect, the source then of so many novelties, though the prince was himself the daring Æneas in search of new kingdoms.

The secretary of the society is Mrs. May St. Clair Whitney-Emerson, only daughter of Levi St. Clair Whitney, whose mother was Mary St. Clair, descended from John Sinclair of Lybster, Reay, fraternal nephew of George, fifth Earl of Caithness. John went from Leith to Exeter, New Hampshire, America, in 1655; and well is he represented by his Emerson descendant among his other kin there. The society by enlarging its borders, on scientific principles of fairness towards feminine descent, to many surnames, does away with a sameness which dims the attractions of British clan societies, such as the Mackay, Fraser, Cameron, and others. Republican generosity

towards men and women generally, as equals before God and the law, is
not offended by genealogical superiorities of catholic width, founded on
actual attainments by energy, blood, or even chance, which rules proverbi-
ally in human affairs. It is a parallel that a Lord Provost of Edinburgh,
John Sinclair, a famous brewer in Leith, the forefather and first baronet,
1636, of the family of Stevenston, Haddingtonshire, and since 1765 also of
Murkle in Caithness-shire, founded a Sinclair society about 1620, noted as
extant well on in the eighteenth century. He died in 1648. A Scotch
song entitled "The Clouting of the Cauldron" was made about the brewer,
who was son of George, the second son of Matthew of Longformacus, who
flourished in 1567, an early offshoot from the Roslin stem, the lairds of
Longformacus baronets till their extinction at the beginning of the nineteenth
century. If, as Hay says, James of Longformacus who, with his son John,
fought at the battle of Homildon Hill in 1401, was the son of the discoverer
of America, the brewer had good traditions from the Longformacus Berwickshire lairds. Another son he supposes to have been the Sir Walter
who was killed in that fight, so fatal to Scots. In 1388, at the battle of
Chevy Chase or Otterburne, Sir Walter and Sir John, brothers, it is thought,
received the last breath of their relative the Douglas, of which scene of
sorrowful affection Froissart, the French chronicler, tells; "Hotspur"
Percy their beaten opponent. Sir John was brother of Prince Henry.

III.

The way is now open to exhibit passages from the life of, at any rate,
by far the greatest of the discoverers, as the world ordinarily calculates
greatness ; and perhaps according to such special worlds as those of history,
literature, and science. In discussing the narrative by the Zeno brothers
from Venice, Fiske says Sir Nicholas Zeno arrived in his ship at the Faroe
Isles, north of Orkney and Shetland, in 1390, only to be shipwrecked.
Prince Henry, who had been invested with his principality by Hacon VI.
of Norway in 1379, was there with thirteen vessels, and succoured the
strangers generously, communicating by speech with them, the narrative
says, in Latin. Sir Antonio Zeno arrived at the Orkneys in 1391, and did
not return to Venice till 1406, during which time the American expeditions

took place. A letter from Sir Antonio to the ambassador, Sir Carlo, another brother in Italy, describes their kind lord as "a prince as worthy of immortal memory as any that ever lived, for his great bravery and remarkable goodness." The above dates authenticate the particular Henry of the Roslin family's lineage who is meant; for there are several of this first name in the line, and like him, men of the highest mark in the affairs of states especially of the north of Europe. He was grandson of Henry the first prince of Orkney of his surname.

His grandfather married Elizabeth, daughter of Julius Sparre, Prince of Orkney, Earl of Caithness, and Earl of Stratherne, through which marriage that Henry became prince. Father Hay, born at Edinburgh, 16th August, 1661, the historian of the family, who was a relative, his mother Jean Spottiswood being first Mrs. Hay, and then lady of the laird of Roslin, had access to the charters of Roslin Castle, and says the prince had power to stamp coin within his dominions, to make laws, and to remit crimes. "He had his sword of honour carried before him wherever he went; he had a crown in his armorial bearings; and he bore a crown on his head when he constituted laws." But Hay's next statement is still more important, the quotation already given from Torfaeus about the grandson, the hero of discovery, corroborated :—" In a word, he was subject to none, except that he held his lands from the kings of Denmark, Sweden, and Norway, and paid homage. To him also it belonged to crown the kings, so that in all those parts he was esteemed second person to the king. He built Kirkwall Castle [demolished 1615], Orkney, and proved valiant in all his doings." The famous letter of the Scotch nobility had his signature at Arbroath in 1320, asking the pope to acknowledge Robert Bruce as king; and he is designed there as *Panetarius Scotiae*, that is, royal or chief baker of Scotland, a household office of state understood by reference to the same under the Pharaoh kings of Egypt. He was governor of the kingdom's corn trade thus. Of the dignity, no easier proof can be given than that Sir Andrew Murray, when husband of a daughter of Robert I., was *Panetarius Scotiae* before it became hereditary to the Earls of Orkney. In Dr. Joseph Anderson's 1873 edition of the "Orkneyinga Saga," with introduction and notes discussing these subjects extensively, there is one piece of information which attaches the discoverer's line early and directly to Caithness events. An Alexander Brown who was an enemy of King Robert Bruce had fled to Orkney, and in 1321 "Henry Sinclair, the king's bailie in Caithness," was commissioned to secure him. This is the *Panetarius Scotiae*, and his crown factorship perhaps explains the first arrival of the Roslins in the regions of the Pentland Firth. Rymer's "Foedera" mentions him as one of the twelve earls of Scotland, "Scotland" then not implying the Orkneys, whose signature Edward II. of England asked in 1323 to the truce of thirteen years between himself and King Robert Bruce; but if, as this implies, and as is said, he had a charter of Caithness, it was resumed by David II. or Robert II., whose son David Stuart had the peerage before 1378. Henry being king's chamberlain of the county, promotion to its earldom was almost a corollary, despite Sir Robert Gordon's weak carping, his wishes the fathers to his thoughts.

This first Prince Henry's son William, was father of the discoverer. William married the eldest daughter of Malise Grahame; from which family came two of Scotland's greatest men, the Marquis of Montrose and Viscount Dundee. Through her, Camden the great antiquary says in his Latin work "Britannia," William, grandson of this William, obtained the earldom of Caithness in 1455; and he is described as *regius panetarius*, the royal baker; the earldom, it would seem, a resumption rather than a new grant. The Grahame earls of Stratherne had rights over Caithness and over lands in Orkney, through marriage with one of the Sparre women, just like the Sinclairs; and they were all near relatives accordingly, with involved positions, some of the male Sparres long contesting the standing of the heiresses, their husbands, and descendants.

IV.

Grahame by his mother, Prince Henry, the navigator to America, has the following written of him by Father Hay :—"He was Prince of Orkney, Lord Sinclair, Lord Zetland, the Lord Chief Justice of Scotland [an office obtained hereditarily by his grandfather], Admiral of the Scottish seas, Lord-warden of the three marches, Lord Nithsdale, baron of Roslin, Pentland, Cousland, Cardan, Herbertshire, Heetfoord, Grahameshaw, Kirkton, and

T

Cavers. He was also Great Protector, Keeper, and Guardian of the Prince of Scotland [as his grandfather was in his time, and his father Prince William, if such care of the crown-prince was hereditary]. He married Egidia Douglas, daughter to Sir William [and niece of one of the several Archibalds who were Earls of Douglas]. The fair Egidia excelled all in her time, grand-daughter to King Robert the Second. Her beauty so dazzled the eyes of beholders that they became presently astonished, but recovered in admiring this princess. Through the marriage, the Prince of Orkney obtained great lands and authority, all the lordship of Nithsdale, the wardenry of the three marches between England and Scotland, the baronies of Heetford, Herbertshire, Grahameshaw, Kirkton, Cavers, and Roxburgh, the sheriffship of Nithsdale, with the provostship of the town of Dumfries. He was a valiant prince, well-proportioned, of middle stature, hasty, and stern."

He had nine sisters, the eldest the Countess of Douglas, the second married to Ramsay of Dalhousie, the third to the laird of Calder, the fourth to Forrester of Corstorphine, the fifth the Countess of Errol, her husband Lord High Constable of Scotland, the sixth wedded to Tweedie of Drumelzier, the seventh to Cockburn of Stirling, the eighth to Herring of Marcton, and the ninth to Lord Somerville. His eldest daughter was Countess of March, and his daughter Beatrix was wife of James, the seventh Earl of Douglas, mother of two Earls of Douglas, of Archibald Douglas the Earl of Murray, of Hugh Douglas the Earl of Ormond, of John Douglas the Lord Balveny, Henry Douglas the Bishop of Dunkeld; her daughters, Margaret, Lady Dalkeith, Janet, Lady Fleming, and Elizabeth Douglas, wife of John Stuart of the royal family, Earl of Buchan and Constable of France. Beatrix's Latin epitaph is extant. Her father, the discoverer, had the greatest part of the nobility his vassals, under bond of manrent, as Lords Salton, Chrichton, Seaton, Dirlton, Halifexburn, Livingstone, Fleming, Borthwick, and Dalkeith, with Foster of Westendry, Preston of Craigmillar, Herring of Gilmerton, Sinclair of Herdmanston, Wauchope of Niddry, and the lairds of Edmiston, Pennycook, Henderleith, Douglas of Pumpherston, and many others. Except Earl Douglas and the Earl of March, most of the Scottish landholders were bound to him.

"He had continually in his house," says Hay, "300 riding gentlemen, and his princess had 55 gentlewomen, of whom 35 were ladies. He had his dainties tasted before him. When he went to Orkney, he had meeting him 300 men with scarlet gowns and coats of black velvet. It was he who built the great dungeon of Roslin Castle, and several walls there. He made parks for fallow and red deer. By King Robert [Stuart] the Third he was much esteemed, and therefore had Prince James, the first of that name, in keeping, lest he should be assassinated by the treason of Robert, Duke of Albany, Earl of Fife and Menteith, who had the whole government of the kingdom. After the king his brother's death, Albany aimed at the crown, for by treason he had slain the king's eldest son, and had thought to do the same to Prince James. Robert the Third, however, before his death, wrote letters to the kings of France and England, stating that his son was to go to the former country for his education ; and he entrusted him, with young Percy, nephew of the Earl of Northumberland, to the Prince of Orkney in 1405 to pass the seas."

" The Book of Cowper," that is, Fordun, says, " The crown-prince stayed at a certain place a short time, when, behold his father the king secretly resolved to send away his dear son, consulting for his safety with a noble man, Henry, Earl of Orkney, and of an honourable family." Leslie in his " History " states that Henry and some other earls were attached to this voyage. Buchanan's account is :—" The ship having been equipped at the Bass, a rock rather than an island [in the Firth of Forth], and Henry Sinclair, Earl of Orkney, appointed its captain, Prince James embarked, and while the vessel hugged the shore near Flamborough Head [in York-shire], either forced by stress of weather, or whether the youth wished to be refreshed a little from sea-sickness, he landed, and was seized by the English ; and, while their king should decide what was to be done about him, he was retained in his palace." Boethius says, " A ship having been made ready, and letters of commendation sent to both kings, that fortune might be met whatever should happen, they set sail from the very strong Bass Castle, under command of Henry, Earl of Orkney, with other nobles accompanying him." King Robert III., reputed bastard like William the Conqueror, is said to have died of grief at the news of the capture and perfidious retention of his son James Stuart in England. But Henry

Fourth, the Usurper, had the grace to educate the youth to the highest possible point; favoured in this by the splendid grounding he had under the hereditary tutor of royalty, Henry, Earl of Orkney, whose castles of Roslin and Kirkwall were historically-acknowledged centres of learning. At Kirkwall Castle particularly, with its neighbouring huge cathedral of St. Magnus and the Bishop's Palace, the crown-prince of Scotland had till his twelfth year the noblest initiation. That he afterwards became the author of "The King's Quhair," a poem hardly second to the best efforts of his contemporary Chaucer, is no wonder at all with such luck of early and later education. The discoverer had all the tales of America to tell to his beloved pupil, for whom he supplied masters in learning of the first European quality. That Henry could speak to the Zenoes in Latin, was indication of at least one section of his scholarly faculty.

But if the future king could be retained in the English court, his guardian was not the man to hug chains of the most gilded kind, but escaped from England. John Robison, indweller at Pentland, and tenant to the Prince of Orkney, came to where his master was imprisoned; and there he played the fool so cunningly, that without any suspicion he was allowed to enter the prison [probably the Tower of London], as often as he pleased. Watching his opportunity, he conveyed the Prince of Orkney outside the gates in disguised apparel prepared for the purpose. They stopped not till they reached a thick forest, where they hid next day, continuing their journey by night, lest they should be taken by their pursuers. They reached the Borders, though the king had put his officers everywhere on the alert. Two southerns there insulted them by asking them to hold their horses, both of whom Prince Henry struck lifeless to the ground [no doubt, after blows on each side in the usual manner of armed quarrel]. When they arrived at Roslin Castle, Robison would take no reward for his devotion. The two other magnates of Scotland, Archibald the Earl of Douglas and George Dunbar the Earl of March, together with all his vassal nobles, at once visited Prince Henry on his return, to congratulate him on his gallant escape. But Robert Stuart, Duke of Albany, the governor of the kingdom, because of hatred for saving the heir to the throne from his hands, accused him of betraying James to the English, and appointed a court to try him for treason, to involve his life and fortunes. Prince Henry promptly met the trick, indignant at such a forged accusation. Collecting great forces, especially from the Zetland and the Orkney isles, he sent an answer to the summons of Regent Albany, that he would certainly appear on the day appointed for his trial, but that one town could not contain them both, without special preparations of lodging for men and stabling for horses. The regent was so offended at this threat and pleasantry, that he had 10,000 men ready in Edinburgh for the day, so as to deal with Prince Henry by force. Having 40,000 men, the latter capped Duke Albany's efforts, who, with three of his officials, fled to Falkland Castle, Fifeshire, where David, Earl of Rothesay, the heir to the throne, Prince James's eldest brother, lost his life. Sinclair, Douglas, and Dunbar then constituted a parliament to depose Albany, and to impeach him for treason as murderer of David, the story running that he had starved him to death. But the regent sent imploring letters and messengers to the triumvirate, who, for the public weal, restored him to office, his skill as a ruler generally admitted, and his crime, if he did it, not provable ; a parliamentary document having pronounced him not responsible for his nephew's death, his enemies ascribing such a finding to the general dread of his ability.

Not long after these events a dispute arose between Henry and his relation Archibald, Earl of Douglas, about the sheriffship of Nithsdale, various lands, and the wardenry of the marches, which he had by his beautiful wife, Egidia Douglas. It rose to such a pitch that Prince Henry would not allow Earl Douglas to ride through his Roslin estates, on his way to the court or capital, Edinburgh. But, says Hay, " for all this, there was no slaughter." There is a complaint in Latin by the princess, as late as 1428, then a dowager, telling the king that she had been despoiled of Nithsdale and its pertinents. She is called the noble and venerable lady, Egidia, Countess of Orkney and Lady of the Vale of Nith ; her son, Prince William of Orkney, backing up the complaint, her brave husband the discoverer then dead.

To return to him, he had his victuals brought by sea from the north, in great abundance, to Roslin Castle. His house was free for all men, so that there was no poor person of his friends who did not receive food and raiment, and no tenant rented to a degree that did not leave him prosperous. "In a word, he was a pattern of piety to all his posterity." To the abbey of Holyrood House, Edinburgh, he gave lands which could support 7000 sheep; and to the service of God, in many churches, he bountifully presented gold, silver, silks, and other materials necessary for beauty of worship. His own relatives were well provided for, his legally able brother John, who married Ingeberg, daughter of Waldemar, King of Denmark, receiving Kirkton, Loganhouse, Earncraig, East and West Summer-Hopes, with other lands. One of his daughters married Dunbar, Earl of March. Beatrix his daughter has been mentioned as Countess of Douglas.

A "History of Sutherland," quoted by Hay, says Henry was Prince of Orkney and Shetland, Duke of Oldenburg in Denmark, Lord Sinclair, Knight of the Cockle of France, Knight of the Order of St. George of England, though it is noted that he is not so enrolled in the register of St. George knights at Windsor. His son William added to these titles Knight of the Golden Fleece of Spain, Lord Chancellor of Scotland, till, by accumulation of an able line, their titles might "weary a Spaniard," as the author carps.

Many further details can be gathered about the discoverer from the "Genealogy" by Father Richard Augustine Hay, Prior of St. Pierremont, France, which work includes in it the chartulary or charters of Roslin. Henry's birth is supposed to have taken place about 1345, and his death certainly was between 1417 and 1428, by two charters recorded in the chartulary, though a nearer dating than this can be fixed gradually hereafter.

V.

His beautiful Douglas was the wife of his old age, which is proved, among other ways, by the fact that the rule of the Orkneys was held by prefects, appointed by the Norwegian crown, till Prince William his son came of age. Thomas Tulloch, Bishop of Orkney, in 1422 was entrusted with the administration of the northern isles by Eric, King of Norway; and the "Book of Cowper" expressly mentions that the second Henry who was count of Orkney died in that year. Another Latin work, by Meursius, says that in 1423 David Manners, a Scotchman, succeeded the bishop in the prefecture. But he ruled so badly that he was ejected from the province, and the government came again into Bishop Tulloch's hands in 1428. It was not, according to Meursius, till 1434 that, in the month of August, King Eric conferred the county of Orkney, under the name of client, upon William Sinclair of the Scottish nobility, and received his homage. Another writer, Pontan, says that Eric the Eighth of Norway on 10th August, 1434, installed William de Sancto Claro, a noble Scotchman, as count of the Orkneys; the implication being that he had then reached age, such a ceremony happening at the accession of each of those princes, as was usual to the feudal system.

Pontan gives the terms of clientship between the king and this prince. The latter was to supply 100 men, fully armed, at three months' notice, when the Norwegian service required soldiers, the king to give them all necessaries in the field. If Orkney and Shetland were invaded, William must collect all forces in the island and defend himself. He was not to build castles and fortresses without agreement of the king. The inhabitants, rich and poor, cleric and lay, would be bridled by the usual laws. Pomona island and its castle of Kirkwall, on William's death, would return to the King of Norway or his successor. This is the usual surrender for the fresh grant to the new heir. There was to be no pledging of the returns obtained from dispensing justice. Little more bond was between them, evidently the amity of feudal subordination all that was meant. Some clauses about not exciting disputes within the domain, and of appealing to the laws of Norway as last resort, with commendation of the clergy to William's care, completed the gentlest of clientships.

The prince's witnesses and cautioners were Henry, Columba, and Robert, bishops respectively of Aberdeen, Apran, and Caithness, the Earls of Douglas, Angus, and March, Sir William Corck, Sir Alexander Ramsay, John Sinclair, and Andrew Chrichton, armsbearing gentlemen. In place of the hostages which his great-grandfather, Henry the First, Prince of the Orkneys, gave to Haco, King of Norway, the seals were accepted of Thomas Sinclair, David Mundtov, Olaf Geton, Alexander Proun, Robert Berion, and John Haroldson, armsbearers. He promised to send copies of his installation writ to the Archbishop of Nidro, Affleck by name, to Thomas

Tulloch, Bishop of Orkney, the governor during his minority, to John, Bishop of Anflo, to Andrew, Bishop of Stavanger, to Peter, Bishop of Hammer, to Olaf, Bishop of Bergen, to Erland, Erlandi, and the rest of knightly and senatorial rank of the kingdom of Norway. King James I. of Scotland stipulated with his uncle, King Eric of Norway, that the royal Scottish seal should be adhibited to these written conditions by William, Earl of Orkney, the document drawn up at Haffnia in Norway.

Both Father Hay and Torfaeus have Latin accounts of the investiture; the former getting his from Pontanus, book 9, p. 596, and the latter his from Scandinavia, where, says the historian, "the whole document is preserved in the royal archives, and a copy was made to me most clemently." The substance of the investitures of all the princes of Orkney is almost the same; showing that the politeness of feudalism meant a formality rather than real bonds, an acknowledgment of comradeship more than any attempt of subordination, beyond what was inevitable. The European system of fee, feu, or feod, at its flowering period of those centuries, was republican in its generosity of, at all events, equality among peers; a sovereign admittedly only the first among his nobles, as with William the Conqueror and his Normans. King Eric and Prince William of Orkney were therefore all but formally equals.

It was the distinguished son of the discoverer of America who became, as is generally reckoned, the first Sinclair Earl of Caithness; his mother's complaint (the beautiful Egidia Douglas, of stature above ordinary, holy of life, excellent in her mind, with a soul of candour, to use the ancient phrases about her), that Nithsdale had been unjustly taken from her, satisfied by the grant to her son of the earldom of Caithness, from James the Second in 1455, in exchange for that beautiful valley, of which Dumfries is now the head town. The same monarch also created him Grand Master of the Freemasons of Scotland, hereditarily, see Mrs. Stowe's "Sunny Memories;" the building of Roslin Gothic chapel, an immortal testimony to his sympathy with the highest architecture. His descendant, the last Baron of Roslin, the model from whom Sir Walter Scott drew his Douglas of "The Lady of the Lake," resigned the honour, as having no male descent, in circumstances of pomp and appreciation at Edinburgh in 1778, for which see *The Scots*

Magazine. Prince William, the discoverer's son, by marriages with a Douglas, and afterwards with a lady of the house of Sutherland, went into the closest affinity with Scottish royalty, beyond even what had been previously. Stoddart mentions that in 1422 the lawmen of Orkney granted attestation in favour of James Craigie, laird of Hope, husband of Margaret, daughter of Henry, Earl of Orkney, by Elizabeth, daughter of Malise, Earl of Orkney, Caithness, and Stratherne. But she was Henry's sister. George Crawford, in his "Lives of the Lord Chancellors of Scotland," published at Edinburgh in 1726, pays the highest tributes, in the biography of Prince William, to his action in this legal office, which he resigned in 1458. His character is suggested by the inscription he had carved with Gothic characters over the door of Roslin Chapel, built by him in 1444, *Forte est vinum, fortior est rex, fortiores sunt mulieres, super omnia vincit veritas*—"Wine is strong, the king is stronger, women are stronger, truth conquers over all." He is written "Lord Chancellor of Scotland" in the confirmation of the earldom of Caithness on 29th April, 1456, by James II., " in compensation of his claim and title to the lordship of Nithsdale, offices, and pensions ;" given to Sir William Douglas, son of Lord Galloway, on his contract of marriage with Giles Stuart, daughter to King Robert the Second by Elizabeth More, and sister to the Regent Albany. This is only one of many affinities of the Sinclairs and the Stuarts ; the connections, through the Grahames, Douglases, and Sparres, of both lineages, closely involved, with respect to persons and estates.

But the purpose is more connected now with the father, Prince Henry, than this William, his son, Scotland and Norway's most powerful subject ; though it is of present day use to notice him as the first recorded Earl of Caithness of his surname. The fair Egidia Douglas had a predecessor as wife of Henry. There is a confirmation by Egidia, Countess of Orkney, Lady of Nithsdale, and Baroness of Herbertshire, of a charter she gave to Livingston of Callendar, Stirlingshire, of the lands of Catsclough, dated 10th September, 1425 ; and it has the combined seal of herself and her husband Henry, the original in the Wigton charter-chest. The American interest of the seal displaying the heraldic shield need not be dwelt upon. The discoverer's arms are on the right, the double tressure indicating his affinity

U

to royalty, the galley of Orkney in the centre, while the engrailed cross is the original Sinclair arms. The princess's arms are the left half of the shield ; the lion of Galloway, in the lower quarter, famous in Douglas blazoning. It was in 1407, 17th September, that Archibald, Earl of Douglas, gave a charter of Herbertshire to Henry, Earl of Orkney, Lord Sinclair, the discoverer, to be held by him and his wife, " my niece ;" the Regent Albany confirming it at Menteith on 20th November, 1407, "the second year of our reign." If this was her portion on occasion of her marriage, it is easy to understand how it was that their son William was not actually ruling as prince of Orkney from 1422 for more than a decade, and how he was not installed till 1434. His birth seems to have been about 1410 to 1413, though it may have been earlier.

On 12th September, 1410, at Roslin, Prince Henry gave a charter to his brother-german, thus described to distinguish that he was not a half-brother, John, of the lands of Sunellis, Hope, and Loganhouse, near Edinburgh, which was ratified under the Great Seal in that city by Regent Albany on 24th September, 1410. Henry, Earl of Orkney, and a Lord William Sinclair signed a charter of Gogar, at Dirleton, 8th June, 1409, which the regent ratified at Falkland Castle, 11th May, 1411. Sir John Forrester of Corstorphine, Edinburgh, to whom one of Henry's daughters was married, had the confirmation about this time of a loan of 300 nobles, receiving 12 merks yearly from Dysart and coals till it was repaid, the sum being the equivalent to £100 sterling, but of much more real value then. Forrester is called "our dearest cousin" in the pledge. At Edinburgh, 10th July, 1424, Henry, Earl of Orkney, resigned Uchtertyre, Perthshire, to Forrester of Corstorphine, as the Register of the Great Seal of Scotland records ; but this date would make his death later than other sources indicate, and it must be a mistake of the printed copies of the register. One of Laing's specimens in his "Scottish Seals" is the seal of Henry, Earl of Orkney, to a charter in favour of Forrester of Corstorphine, of date 26th November, 1407, and the charter of Uchtertyre must have been also earlier than 1424.

In a procuration to the same brother John dated Edinburgh, 1411, 10th November, Henry is called Earl of Orkney and Lord Sinclair and

Lord Nithsdale ; so that the last title came through his wife after the charter of the lands of Herbertshire. That he was old in 1411, this deputing or procuratory of his business to his " very dear brother-german," the skilful John, son-in-law to the King of Denmark, and brother-in-law to Hagen, the King of Norway, may be an indication. An amnesty document between Henry and his relative Malise Sparre, in 1387, on 8th November, signed at Edinburgh, describes him then as Earl of Orkney and Lord of Roslin ; so that the Douglas marriage was certainly subsequent to that date.

By the " Book of Cowper " a William died in 1422, the same year in which Prince Henry's death took place ; and the inference is that they were father and son. Henry had a son Lord William mentioned in the Gogar charter above of 1409 by his first marriage, as he had Prince William by his Douglas wife. The first William dying by disease in 1422, opened the succession to his half-brother William, then a boy of perhaps eleven. Nor is this mere inference, which is always dangerous in historical fields. Father Hay says that it is certain that Henry was " sent ambassador to Copenhagen, Denmark, in 1363, where there was a marriage celebrated between Margaret, daughter to Waldemar, King of Denmark, and Hagen, King of Norway." About the same time he had a confirmation of the lands of Orkney ; no doubt, when he came of age, or soon after. His procurators had to receive it, as he was himself too ill to go to Norway for the purpose.

We gather from these dates that the discoverer was born about 1340 and died in 1422, so that he reached longevity of more than eighty years, a family characteristic. But in a genealogy of the Stuarts published in the end of the last century written by Andrew Stuart, M.P., there is a dispensation extracted from the records in the Vatican, Rome, which would make Henry's death earlier. It was given by Pope Martin V., the year after accession, on the 3rd of the Kalends of April, 1418, to Egidia Douglas, widow of Sir Henry Sinclair, and to Alexander Stuart, who could not marry without it, being in second and third degrees of affinity, the marriage to quiet family rancours. This would make 1417 the probable date of the discoverer's death, at the latest, if the dispensation was copied correctly. A similar dispensation from Innocent VI., at Avignon, the year after his appointment, was given in 1353 to Thomas Stuart, Earl of Angus, and Margaret Sinclair, "a noble lady," of the Roslin family so much interknit with the royal Stuarts. This Earl of Angus took Berwick from the English, see Buchanan, page 259, before the Stuarts were kings.

On Prince Henry's installation "there was a marriage concluded between the Earl and King Hagen's sister, who was daughter to Magnus, King of Sweden and Norway." We know, therefore, the first wife of the discoverer of America; and it is a safe conclusion that through her the Roslins became Dukes of Oldenburg, then belonging to Denmark, the duchy her marriage portion. She is named Florentia in various books; and had, it would seem, an only son, the Lord William who died the same year as his father, but several daughters, who married into the Scotch and Scandinavian nobility.

VI.

Queen Margaret of Norway's son, by Wartislaus, Duke of Pomerania, was proclaimed nearest heir to the crown of Norway in 1388 by Prince Henry, as already said; but Pontan, "a most accurate writer of Danish affairs," gives numerous details in addition about the letters by the archbishop, bishops, and nobles of that kingdom, backing up Henry's official declaration, sent everywhere for authenticating Eric's standing, according to the Norwegian laws.

Pontan also records the circumstances of Henry's installation in 1379 over the Orkneys. About the third of the Ides of June, there came to King Hagen of Norway, William Dalziel, Malise Sparre, and Alexander Ard, as commissioners from Henry, Earl of Orkney, with cautionry as client for the islands of that principality, according to feudal custom. A writ which was finished at Malstrand about Prince Henry, had been altered before being signed by the Scotch earls and barons; and King Hagen refused to sanction it at first; but when the commissioners had stayed some time at Tesberge city in Norway, the king after fresh changes ratified the agreement. The commissioners promised 1000 golden nobles, coins worth 6s. 8d. sterling each, as, apparently, an annual gift of complacency on Henry's part.

The document is in full in Torfaeus's "Orcades," and, translated from Latin, will follow after this from him, "In the year 1369, Count Henry Sinclair was by fiduciary right set over the Orkneys. He, sending ambassadors to King Hacon in the Ides of June, demanded the administration of the fee to be confirmed to him, which under fixed conditions he obtained in 1370." For some unknown reason of rebellion or wars, he was supplanted in 1375 by his relative Alexander Ard, who had also descent from Sparres or Spiers, the Scotch favourite or minion, and the former prince ; but in 1379, King Hacon established Henry over the Orkneys, renewed his title of count, gave and received mutual letters of elaborate extent, and accepted the oath of fealty or homage in the usual manner. The translation of Prince Henry's obligation or agreement is :—

"To all who shall see or hear the present letters Henry, Earl of the Orkneys, Lord of Roslin, wishes salvation in the Lord. Because the very serene prince in Christ, my most clement lord, Haquin, by the grace of God the king of the kingdoms of Norway and Sweden, has set us by his favour over the Orcadian lands and islands, and has raised us into the rank of jarl over the beforesaid lands and islands, and since this is required by the dignity, we make well known to all, as well to posterity as to contemporaries, that we have made homage of fidelity to our lord the king himself, at the kiss of his hand and mouth, and have given to him a true and due oath of fidelity, as far as counsels and aids to our same lord the king, his heirs, and successors, and to his kingdom of Norway, must be observed. And so, let it be open to all that we and our friends, whose names are expressed lower, have firmly promised in faith and with our honour to our same lord the king, and to his men and councillors, that we must faithfully fulfil all agreements, conditions, promises, and articles which are contained in the present letters to our beforesaid lord the king, his heirs, and successors, and to his kingdom of Norway.

"In the first place, therefore, we firmly oblige us to serve our lord the king outside of the lands and islands of the Orkneys, with 100 good men or more, equipped in complete arms, for the conveniences and use of our same lord the king, whenever we shall have been sufficiently requisitioned by his messengers or his letters, and forewarned within Orkney three months. But when the men shall have arrived in the presence of our lord the king, from that time he will provide about victuals for us and ours.

"Again, if any may wish to attack or hostilely to invade, in manner whatsoever, the lands and islands of the Orkneys, or the land of Zetland, then we promise and oblige us to defend the lands named, with men whom we may be able to collect in good condition for this solely, from the lands and islands themselves, yea, with all the force of relatives, friends, and servants.

" Also, if it shall be necessary that our lord the king attack any lands or any kingdoms, by right or from any other reason or necessity, then we shall be to him in help and service with all our force.

" Moreover, we promise in good faith that we must not build or construct castles or any fortifications within the lands and islands beforesaid, unless we shall have obtained the favour, good-pleasure, and consent of our same lord the king.

" We also shall be bound to hold and to cherish the said lands and islands of the Orkneys, and all their inhabitants, clergymen and laity, rich and poor, in their rights.

" Further, we promise in good faith that we must not at any time sell or alienate that beforesaid county and that lordship, whether lands or islands, belonging to the earldom, or our right which we obtain now to the earldom, the lands, and islands, by the grace of God and of the king our lord, from our lord the king himself, or his heirs, and successors, or from the kingdom, nor to deliver these or any of these for surety and for pledge to any one, or to expose them otherwise, against the will and good-pleasure of him and his successors.

" In addition, if it happen that our lord the king, his heirs, or successors wish to approach those lands and islands for their defence, or from other reasonable cause, or to direct thither his councillors or men, then we shall be held to be for help to our same lord the king, and his heirs, to his councillors and men, with all our force, and to minister to our lord the king, and his heirs, his men and councillors, those things of which they may be in need for their due expenses, and as necessity then requires, at least to ordain so from the lands and islands.

" Moreover, we promise that we must begin or rouse no war, law suit, or dissension with any strangers or natives, by reason of which war, law suit, or dissension the king my lord, his heirs, or successors, or their kingdom of Norway, or the beforesaid lands and islands, may receive any damage.

" Again, if it happen, but may this be absent, that we notably and unjustly do wrong against any within the beforesaid lands and islands, or inflict some notable injury upon any one, as the loss of life, or mutilation of limbs, or depredation of goods, then we shall answer to the pursuer of a cause of that kind in the presence of our lord the king himself and his councillors, and satisfy for the wrongs according to the laws of the kingdom.

" Also, whensoever our lord the king shall have summoned us, on account of any causes, to his presence, where and when he shall have wished to hold his general assembly, then we are bound to go to him, to give him advice and assistance.

" Further, we promise that we shall not break the truces and security of our same lord the king, nor his peace, which he shall have made or confirmed with foreigners or natives, or with whomsoever others, in any manner whatever, to violate them, nay, defend them all as far as our strength, and hold those as federated to us whom the king of Norway himself, our lord, may wish to treat as his favourers and friends.

" We promise also that we must make no league with the Orcadian bishop, nor enter into or establish any friendship with him, unless from the good-pleasure and consent of our lord the king himself ; but we must be for help to him against that bishop, until he shall have done to him what is of right, or shall be bound to do so for that special reason, upon those things in which my lord the king may wish or be able reasonably to accuse that bishop.

" Besides, when God may have willed to call us from life, then that earl-dom and that lordship, with the lands and islands, and with all the jurisdiction, must return to our lord the king, his heirs and successors freely ; and if we shall have children after us, procreated from our body, male, one or more, then he of them who shall claim the above said carldom and lordship must demand, with regard to this, the favour, good-pleasure, and consent of our lord the king himself, his heirs, and successors.

" Further, we promise in good faith that we shall be bound to pay to our abovesaid lord the king, or to his official at Tunisberg, on the next festival of St. Martin the bishop and confessor, a thousand golden pieces, which are called nobles, of English money, in which we acknowledge us to be bound to him by just payment.

" Also, we promise, because we have been now promoted to the carldom and lordship oftensaid by our lord the king himself, that our cousin Malise Sparre must cease from his claim and dismiss altogether his right, if it be discernible that he has any, to those lands and islands ; so that my lord the king, his heirs, and successors shall sustain no vexation or trouble from him or from his heirs.

" Again, if we have made any agreement or any understanding with our cousin Alexander Ard, or have wished to enter into any treaty with him, in that case we will do similarly on our part and on the part of the king my lord to whatever was done in precaution about Malise Sparre.

" Further, we, Henry, earl abovesaid, and our friends and relatives within-written, namely, Simon Rodde, William Daniels, knights, Malise Sparre, William Chrichton, David Chrichton, Adam Byketon, Thomas Bennine, and Andrew Haldaniston, armsbearers, conjunctly promise in good faith to our oftensaid lord the king, Haquin, and to his first-born lord the king, Olaf, and to his councillors and men within-written, namely, to the lords Signard, Haffthorsen, Ogmund Findersen, Eric Ketelsen, Narvo Ingualdisen, John Oddosen, Ulpho Johnsen, Ginther de Vedhonsen ; John Danisen, Haquin Evidassen, knights of the same lord the king ; Haquin Jonssen, Alver Hardlssen, Hantho Ericsen, Erlend Phil-lippsen, and Otho Remer, armsbearers ; and for this, under preservation of our honour, we bind ourselves and each of us in a body to the aforesaid lords, that we must truly and firmly fulfil all the agreements and conditions and articles which are expressed above to our lord the king, within the above-written feast of St. Martin the bishop and confessor, so far as one particular business was declared by itself above.

"That all these things now promised may have the greater strength for this, and may be fulfilled the sooner, we, the aforesaid Henry, Earl of the Orkneys, place and leave behind us our cousins and friends Lord William Daniels, knight, Malise Sperre, David Chrichton, and the lawful son of the said Simon, by name Lord Alexander, here in the kingdom hostages. Upon their faith they oblige and promise themselves to this, that from our lord the king of Norway, or from that place in which he shall have wished to have them within his kingdom of Norway, they in nowise may go away, publicly or secretly, before all the abovesaid things be totally fulfilled with entire integrity to our lord the king; and particularly and specially, the conditions and articles for whose observation the within-written reverend fathers, bishops, and prelates of the churches of the kingdom of Scotland, and the other nobles within-written of the same kingdom, Lord William, Bishop of St. Andrews; Lord Walter, Bishop of Glasgow; Lord William, Earl of Douglas; Lord George, Earl of March; Lord Patrick Hepburn, Lord Alexander Haliburton, Lord George Abernethy, Lord William Ramsay, knights, must promise in good faith, and upon this remit their open letters to our same king the lord, with their true seals, in the before-noted time, as in our other letters written upon this is declared more fully.

"Also, we promise in good faith that we must assume in no direction to us the lands of our lord the king, or any other rights of his which his progenitors and the king our lord are known to have reserved to themselves; and concerning those lands or jurisdictions not to intromit in any manner whatsoever. They have reserved those laws, indeed, and those pleas within the Orcadian earldom, as is before said, and the lands and pleas of that kind will remain in all cases safe for them; but if, upon this, we shall have his special letters, then we ought to be specially bound thereafter to our same lord the king.

"Besides, but may it be absent, if all those abovesaid things shall not have been brought to conclusion, and totally fulfilled to the same my lord the king as it has been expressed above, or if we should have attempted anything in the contrary of any of the premises, then the promotion and favour which we have experienced from the king our lord, and of his grace, ought to be of no strength; yea, the promotion and favour of that kind done to us must be broken down altogether, and in their forces be totally empty and inane, so that we and our heirs for the rest shall have no right of speaking for the beforesaid county or for the lands or beforesaid islands, or we of acting about those lands and islands in any way whatsoever, that it may be manifest to all that the promotion and grace of this kind was given by no force of law or justice.

"And so we append our seal, together with the seals of our said friends, to our present letters, in testimony and the firmer evidence of all the premises.

"These things were done at Marstrand, in the year of the Lord 1379, the 2nd day of August."

There is the other obligation given at St. Andrews, Scotland, on 1st September, 1379, by *Henricus de Sancto Claro, Comes Orchadiae, Dominus de Roslin in Scotia*, to use the Latin, not to mortgage the earldom of Orkney without King Haquin's consent, practically of the same tenor as one of the clauses in the document above translated. It was signed and sealed by the same persons, with the addition of Sir Walter Haliburton, Sir John Edmonston, Sir Robert Dalyell, Sir John Thumbee. These deeds were not of installation ; for Prince Henry had at least sixteen years previously come to age and occupancy. They are of the nature of a fresh feudal confirmation by the sovereign of Norway, on occasion of accession to his crown, or quelled disputing about the right to Orkney and Shetland ; the fixing of a tribute of 1000 gold nobles upon Henry suggesting the latter alternative. The following is the text from Torfaeus :—

"Henry Sinclair, Earl of Orkney, Lord of Roslin in Scotland, salvation in the Saviour of all. We make well known to your entirety, by the presents, that we have promised in good faith, and by the tenor of the presents we promise with all fidelity, to our most excellent prince and lord the lord Haquin, the illustrious King of Norway and Sweden, that we will alienate, pledge, or deliver as surety on no account the lands or islands of the county of Orkney, or the crown possessions of the kingdom itself, from our beforesaid lord the king, his successors, or from the kingdom, without the consent of our lord the king abovesaid, his heirs, or successors, and that we shall observe faithfully all the premises.

"The venerable lords and fathers in Christ, Lords William and Walter, Bishops of St. Andrews and Glasgow ; William and George, Earls of Douglas and March ; William Ramsay, Walter Haliburton, George Abernethy, Patrick Hepburn, John Edmonston, Alexander Haliburton, John Thumbee, Robert Dalzell, barons and knights, also have promised.

"In testimony of all which things our seal was appended, and we have procured to be appended to the presents the seals of the said bishops, counts, barons, and knights.

"Given at St. Andrews on the first day of the month of September, 1379."

VII.

Through the Sparre and Grahame heiresses, the four earldoms of Caithness, Orkney, Stratherne, and Menteith had gone to the Rosses, the Sinclairs, the Grahames, and the royal Stuarts, creating the most involved rivalries between these close kinsfolk. In 1373, six years before Prince

V

Henry signed his Orkney homage document to King Haquin of Norway, David Stuart, the son of Robert II. by his queen Euphemia Ross, Earl of Stratherne, became Earl of Caithness, with Braal Castle the head messuage. His mother was heiress of the Earls of Ross, who had had Caithness earldom through marrying a Grahame heiress, sister of Prince Henry's mother. David's brother, Walter, Earl of Athole, became also Earl of Caithness, whose son Allan was the last of the royal Stuart Earls of Caithness, and slain in battle in 1426 after two years' possession. The very heart and knot of British history are to be found in these extraordinary relationships. The Caithness Stuarts were the lawful line of Robert II.; but he dispossessed them, by parliamentary resolution, in favour of his reputed bastard children by his concubine, Elizabeth More. Their indignation and that of their relatives, the Grahames, culminated in the murder of James the First of Scotland in 1437, at Perth; Walter Stuart and Sir Robert Grahame executed, with tortures, for their violent form of trying to vindicate justice to the lawful heirs of the throne. By the common law of Britain, all the reigning royal Stuarts, except Robert the Second, who began the dynasty, were and are illegitimate; the ruler of the British empire holding office on this sandy descent foundation, if use and wont or accomplished fact, as history exemplifies largely, be not enough for establishing regal possession. In the time of Prince Henry the controversy between the lawful and unlawful or semi-lawful Stuarts had not reached the acute stage; but all the tragic elements were at work; the Douglas higher rights to the crown, through heiring the Comyns, who claimed fairly to come before the Bruce kings, by whom the Stuarts inherited, still further complicating the problem of the notoriously unfortunate and, it is all but assured, false dynasty which has played so extraordinary a part in Scotch, English, and Irish history. Through the Earl of Ross's connection with the Sinclairs, by the Grahame and Sparre heiresses, Henry, Earl of Orkney, might be expected to favour Queen Euphemia Ross's Stuart children and descendants, certainly a lawful line; but canonical and civil law making the concubine's children legitimate through a subsequent marriage to King Robert II., if it occurred, and the eldest of them, afterwards Robert III., having been declared by parliament to be crown-prince, the important men of the kingdom could not help themselves, least of all Henry, who was hereditary guardian of the heirs to the throne. Though the best material as to spirit and body, young Prince James Stuart must have seemed in Kirkwall Castle a doubtful falcon to train, the son of a "light-of-love" beauty. His tragic death is no wonder at all to those able to see into the seething caldron of rivalries and injustices about the end of the fourteenth and beginning of the fifteenth century in Scotland. For the law consult the *Majestatem*, II., 51.

But to come to Henry's own immediate difficulties. It is clear that both Ard and a collateral or illegitimate representative of the Sparres from whom Orkney came to the Sinclairs, had designs upon his principality, his "cousins" of the document translated above. The Ards had wide lands in Inverness-shire and other counties of Scotland, through marriage to one of the heiresses so often, but not too often, mentioned, considering their unusual importance; and in the national records Ards are principal persons. They, however, died out, and only the Sparres, originally of southern Scotland, were troublers of Henry's position, probably contending that the fee ought to have gone to the males of the Sparre family, though feudalism freely parted estates among females in all parts of Europe. But there may have been a special enactment as to males, or a variation in Norse tenures, from need of leaders in war, as it was in the bastard Celtic feudalism of West Scotland and Ireland. At all events, Torfaeus shows that matters came to violence between Sinclair and a false or true rival from the Sparre or Spier family :—" In the year 1391, the Earl of Orkney slew Malise Sparre, in Zetland, with seven others. A young man, however, with six followers, having found a ship, escaped by flight to Norway." By the Register of the Great Seal of Scotland, Henry, Earl of Orkney, gave to Sir David, his half-brother, for his rights in Orkney and Shetland, through his mother Isabella, all the lands of Newburgh and Auchdale, Aberdeenshire, the charter dated Kirkwall, 23rd April, 1391, the properties to return to Henry if David died childless, Robert III. ratifying it at Rothesay Castle, 10th June, 1392. It is evident that the prince was consolidating his power in the Orkneys against all comers, probably the Sparre disorder going on at the very moment of the grant or exchange. That the slaughter of his ambitious cousin was no hasty or tyrannical proceeding on Prince Henry's part, is proved by the following :—

" *Amends of Malise Sparre made to Henry, Earl of Orkney* :—To all to whose knowledge the present letters shall have arrived Malise Sper, Lord of Skuldale, salvation in the Saviour of all. Let your entirety know that I have made, in the presence of a magnificent lord, James, Earl of Douglas, firm friendship with Henry Sinclair, Earl of Orkney and Baron of Roslin, and have condoned and remitted finally all actions of injuries and offences, by him, his men, or whomsoever in his name, to my men, lands, and possessions whatsoever, and as to his universal goods, acquired by him or his. Further, I firmly promise to restore, pay, and satisfy, with my men whomsoever, concerning all injuries, offences, and things acquired, as to the beforesaid Lord Earl, or whomsoever in his name, up to the present day, with lands and possessions excepted, if there are any to which my men have the right of claiming according to the laws of the country. In testimony of this transaction, my seal was appended to the presents at Edinburgh, 18th November, 1387."

The treaty did not last long ; for four years later the struggle between the cousins ended in Sparre's death, after a period of open war and blood-shed, and also rebellion ; the last, because Prince Henry had investiture by the Norwegian crown in 1379, Malise Sparre himself one of the principal persons at the installation, and waiving all rights.

VIII.

While thus effectually quelling the Sparre insurrection with thirteen war-vessels, Prince Henry met at the Faroe Isles Sir Nicolas Zeno, the Venetian navigating noble, who had suffered shipwreck there. It was in 1390 that Sir Nicolas passed through the Straits of Gibraltar, on the way to the northern seas for discovery, according to the analysis by Major, the American admirer of Prince Zichmni and the celebrated Zenoes. Carlo of them was grand admiral of Venice, the ambassador to England, and died 8th May, 1418 ; Raniero was doge of Venice, dying in 1268 : Caterino went ambassador to Persia in 1472 ; James was an Italian orator (1417-81), and another of the Zeno lineage was Nicholas, junior, the biographer of Prince Henry's two brother admirals, he born in 1515, and dying 10th August, 1565, to whom Americans owe the earliest civilised chapter of their history. Bancroft gives only his first page to the Norse discoverers (not

mentioning Prince Henry and the Zenoes at all, Columbus getting his whole
enthusiasm) in the "History of the United States;" the Scandinavians
scantily credited, though Humboldt in his "Cosmos," Malte - Brun the
great geographer, Rafn, and a world of other authorities accepted the early
voyages and discoveries. Torfaeus's "Vinlandia Antiqua," published at
Hafn in 1705, of itself puts the question out of the region of probabilities,
Vinland being Boston "and all around it." The ninth edition of the
"Encyclopædia Britannica" receives the Norse rovers as historic verities.
Sir Antonio Zeno arrived at the Orkneys in 1391, and assisted his brother
Sir Nicholas, who was admiral of Prince Henry's fleet, "in taking possession of Zetland islands," clearly the Sparre attempt put down. So
notable because undesigned an agreement of Torfaeus with the "Lives" of
the Zeno brothers, attests the veracity of the biographical work, which is
now beyond criticism, though from Pinkerton in his "History of Scotland,"
1797, till of late, it had to stand a considerably hostile and, because of
prevailing ignorance, misdirected fire of objections.

The American expeditions followed the Zetland subjugation; and it is
a hopeful statement for the De Sancto Claro Society to investigate, that
from the time when Prince Henry first annexed America to his principality
(for such is the technicality of the proceeding), that continent never lost
white representatives to this day. Norse and Scotch were hardly the kind
of people to neglect the possession of lands, not to say kingdoms; and there
is no proof that they did not, again and again, plant colonists whose
descendants are now in New England and on other parts of the Atlantic
shore. White men would have thus been continuous in America from the
ninth century till now, a most interesting problem to authenticate. It is
true that Prince Henry, according to the Zeno biography, gave up at one
time a colony there; but the book does not come to the close of his
life: and he and his great-hearted son, Prince William of Orkney, Lord
Nithsdale, Baron of Roslin, and the first recorded Earl of Caithness of his
surname, were not the men to be baulked of their high objects. A land
without limit like America, would appeal to their heroic persistency: and it
is almost assured that they repeated again and again their occupation of the
continent. Everyone knows of the traditional rumours that Christian

bishops were among the Red Indians, some ascribing their advent to Ireland, some to Wales, whose Celtic books are full of a western land beyond the seas in much earlier centuries than those of Prince Henry and Prince William. It is most akin to historical fact that the clerical and laic white men of Indian legend, were colonists and conquerors from Scandinavia and Scotland; the annexing of savage kingdoms to the church of the pope being, especially in the 14th and 15th centuries, a positive madness of the brain. The Spaniards led by Columbus thought more of the conversion of the Indians to Christianity than they did of gold, though of this they are credited to have been supreme lovers. Later, Mexico and Peru had to be saved, and such salvation! The former, it is true, was by priest-sanctioned cannibalism a pandemonium of blood; and Christian fire may have purified that cookery horror off the face of the earth, as moral sanitation. The New England districts have yet a tale to tell, of Europeans, a century earlier than the Spaniards, carrying the religious and material civilisation of Europe and Asia there; and it may be provable that the remnant never died out, though the puritans of the "May Flower" claim to have been the pioneers of Yankeeland or Englishland. Englishmen, at all periods, have had the useful trick of assuming too much in their own favour; and the nonconformists who left old Plymouth of England to found the new Plymouth of America, had enough of this valuable quality of Emerson's self-reliance about 1620, when they fled from Archbishop Laud's ecclesiastical tyranny, to forget that there were whites there long before them. Indeed, the marvellously developed social condition of the Red Indians, with their communal long houses, suggests Norwegian and Scottish training grafted on mere savagery. Fiske exhibits the Delawares and the rest of the native tribes, or six nations or more, in lights absolutely novel to those with the preconceived ideas obtained from Fenimore Cooper's romantic novels. But enough, in so untrodden but not unpromising field. The De Sancto Claro Society has, however, inquiries and successes in this direction also, as nothing has been more striking than recent American advance in knowledge of the primitive races; scientific precision by and bye perhaps to be able to distinguish external influences over their highly-articulated popular life. Celtic and Norse literature is full of shadowings of ancient intercourse from Europe to America; and such dreamings nearly always, in research, prove to be founded on facts of some extent. The want of historians and the accidents of time have blotted out many a chapter of human experience, now beyond our imagination to fathom; but the acuteness of learning recovers wonderful gold-dust from the river of the past, which becomes in due time coin and currency. It is already pretty certain that the Norse and Scotch heroes left a sprinkling of population, who ruled the Red Indians to some extent, and amalgamated with them. The French half-breeds of Canada show how it could have been done; for before the " brave " was taught the use of gunpowder, he was not the cruel intractable creature with whom the modern mind is familiar. Who is not aware of the freedom with which missionaries went from tribe to tribe in the earlier European periods of America? One lay stranger was so beloved by them that he was called universally their " father." He, Dr. Patrick Sinclair, was only one of many, from others, too, than the English and Scotch, who experienced ease in guiding these so-called savages; the French at all times most insinuating and charming visitors, whom they never tired of welcoming, with whatever excess or want of wisdom.

IX.

Torfaeus quotes Buchanan, the historian of Scotland, that Prince Henry was entrusted with James, the then eldest son of Robert the Third, to take him for safety and education to France in 1406, Hay saying 1404. Consulting Buchanan, Torfaeus seems to be right, because the king expired of grief three days after hearing of his only remaining son being taken by the English. He died at Rothesay on the Clyde, the tenth of the Kalends of April, 1406; and the news could not have taken months, not to say two years, to arrive. " In the year 1418," Torfaeus writes, " John Sinclair professed himself, with all Shetland, the client of King Eric Pomeranus; " a most interesting note, because this is Prince Henry's learned statesman brother, who had married the daughter of Waldemar, King of Denmark. In his old age, evidently Prince Henry grew specially generous, thus giving the lordship of Shetland to his brother. Another brother, Thomas, was the mandatory of Prince Henry to look after the interests of his son Prince

William, a minor at his father's death in 1420; and he took a principal
part in ejecting David Manners from Orkney and Shetland, who had secured
the prefecture from King Eric, equivalent to a "gift of nonentry," in terms
of Scotch law about landed property. While the heir was under age, the
crown could traffic with the rents more or less. But the youth's uncle
proved faithful to his mandate, and Torfaeus tells much of Thomas's energetic and skilful doings. His servants were beaten and imprisoned by
Manners, who took the money of returns belonging to his family by force,
and who oppressed everybody, especially the supporters of the mandatory;
but he laughs best who laughs last; and the tyrannical intruder was driven
away from the Orkneys by popular indignation. Torfaeus details thirty-
five crimes with which he was charged as a prefect during his five years of
rule. Thomas Sinclair's seal was the first appended to the installation
document of Prince William in 1434, when he paid feudal homage, after
the manner of the Scotch to the English kings, to Eric, King of Norway,
Denmark, and Sweden. Eric is so designed in Bishop Tulloch's appointment to succeed Manners in the prefecture in 1427, of which document
Torfaeus gives a copy, Tulloch holding the diocese of the Orkneys. Stoddart says that in 1364 a Thomas Sinclair was *ballivus regis Norvagiae*,
that is, "bailie of the King of Norway," in Orkney; but if this date is right,
there must have been two of the name, with similar offices.

In a Latin index to an edition of "*Rerum Scoticarum Historia*," by
George Buchanan (1506-82), published by John Paton, Edinburgh, in 1727,
at 5s. 6d., the editor, Robert Fribarn, the following occurs :—*Sinclarus,
Sinclair, St. Clare, cognomen illustris familiae, quorum Principes olim
Orcadum et Cathanesiae Comites ; nunc Sinclariae Reguli primi existi-
mantur*—"Sinclare, Sinclair, St. Clare, the surname of an illustrious family,
of whom the heads were formerly the Princes of Orkney and the Earls of
Caithness; but now the Lords of Sinclair are thought the first." It is
always the more valuable to have such references from others than the
lineage, like this learned Fribarn; because there is no suspicion of partiality
or prejudice. The Scottish parliament passed an act on 26th January,
1488-9, that Sir Henry, the eldest son of Prince William, was chief of that
blood, and was to be called Lord Sinclair thereafter. His male descent

died out in John, the seventh lord, in 1676; and then the Earls of Caithness became, and still are, the heads of the name. His only daughter
Catherine married John Sinclair of Herdmanston, Haddingtonshire, of a
very ancient baronial family, but of no known male relationship to the
Roslins. The present peer, Lord Sinclair, is of the Herdmanston family,
noted for its ability and learning. It will be remarked, therefore, that
Fribarn made a mistake in saying that his contemporary Lord Sinclair was
the first then of the surname, that honour having passed to the Earl of
Caithness fifty-one years before.

Dr. James Wallace in his "Account of the Islands of Orkney," pub-
lished at London in 1700, says Henry was usually called the Prince of
Orkney, and that he was also made Duke of Oldenburg by Christian I. of
Denmark, thus doubly prince. See chapter I. *infra*.

In John Entick's "Present State of the British Empire," which
description included the United States as British colonies, the book published in 1774 at London, there is good knowledge thus:—"The Orkneys
had formerly their own kings, till subdued by Kenneth McAlpin, King of
Scotland, about the year 840; but not resting quiet under the conqueror,
Donald Bane, King of Scotland, in the year 1009, took the opportunity to
get rid of them, by giving the Orkneys up to the King of Norway for assist-
ing him in his usurpation. Under this authority the Norwegians invaded
the Orkneys, reduced them to their obedience, and kept possession for 164
years, when Magnus, King of Norway, sold them to Alexander, King of
Scotland, who granted the property of all these islands to his favourite
Speire, from whom it descended in the female line to the Sinclairs or St.
Clares; one of whom married the daughter of the King of Denmark, and
was honoured with the titles of Prince of Orkney, Duke Oldenburg, &c."
Speire, Sper, Sparre, and Sparres, as well as the mistaken or evil spelling
of Sware by Sir Robert Gordon in his "Genealogy of the Earls of Suther-
land," mean the same family of the favourite, a southern Scotchman.

X.

A Latin diploma, dated 1st June, 1406, at Kirkwall, by Thomas Tulloch,
Bishop of Orkney, and by the chapter of the cathedral of Kirkwall, which

W

was addressed to Eric, King of Norway, gives the genealogy of Prince William, son of Prince Henry, the discoverer of America, and the latter has his paragraphs in it. See for this invaluable official document vol. 3 of "The Bannatyne Miscellany," published 1827. The first translator of it from the Latin was T. Guild in 1554, a Newbottle monk. The famous author of "Satan's Invisible World Discovered" (not America), George Sinclair, professor of Natural Philosophy, Glasgow University, appointed 1672, afterwards minister of Eastwood, Renfrewshire, has a genealogical preface to one of his books. Alexander Nisbet, the herald, in his "Memorial of the Ancient Family of Sinclair of Roslin," says that it was Sir Henry of the Bruce and Baliol wars (the successful battle of Edward Baliol at Dupplin taking place in 1332) who "married Florentia, daughter of the King of Denmark, with whom he got a great estate in Norway; and from his mother he had Zetland and Orkney." Of the discoverer he says that he was "Knight of the Thistle, Knight of the Cockle, and Knight of the Golden Fleece; and married, as second wife, the fair Egidia, the grand-daughter of Robert II." Of his son Prince William he says he was Duke of Oldenburg in Denmark, and "the greatest subject by far of all others of his time," whose daughter "Helen was married to the Duke of Albany, heir-presumptive, as nearest Stuart, to the throne of Scotland." In another passage this noted Scotch genealogist says, "Henricus de Sancto Claro, heir of the great family of the Sinclairs of Roslin, who not only overtopped the other families of Sinclairs who were equal to them in antiquity, but most of the noble families in the kingdom, for they were Earls of Orkney and then of Caithness;" and again, in describing the Herdmanstons, he says John "was married with the other ancient but far more powerful family of the Sinclairs of Roslin, who in truth exceeded most other families in the kingdom for grandeur and wealth." He thinks that Gregory of Long-formacus, who appears in 1384, was a brother of Prince Henry, the discoverer of Vinland. Daniel Defoe, the author of "Robinson Crusoe," in his "Travels and Guide Book," says, "The Sinclairs lost the Orkneys and Shetlands by the extravagance of William the Waster, as he was called. They got those through marrying their heiress, a Speire. Lord Ravensheuch of Fifeshire was the head of the family." With a rider as to the real facts about William, these references of the Englishman are good. The marriage to the Speire lady took place in 1331 ; and her husband paid homage for the territories he had with her to Haco, King of Norway, soon after the happy event.

In his "History of the Mackays," 1829, Robert Mackay has a detailed account, taken chiefly from Bishop Tulloch's diploma, printed in 1827. Magnus, Earl of Orkney and Caithness, who signed the letter to the pope in 1320, was the last, he says, of the Danish line descended from Rognvald, Earl of Möre, Norway, and had only one child, a daughter. She married Julius Spier or Spar, the king's favourite, Earl of Strathearne, afterwards a palatine county. Their heiress daughter married Malise Grahame, the Earl of Stratherne, through her right. Their eldest son, Malise, married, first, a daughter of the Earl of Menteith, by whom he had a daughter only, Matilda Grahame, the wife of Wayland Ard. He married, secondly, a daughter of Hugh, Earl of Ross, by whom he had four daughters, the eldest of whom married Lord William, the baron of Roslin. By Wayland Ard Matilda had a son, Alexander Ard, who in his mother's right became Earl of Caithness, and held rights over part of Orkney, but who alienated all to Robert II., the first Stuart King of Scotland, dying without heir. It was his claims to Orkney that the second Prince Henry, at his investiture in 1379, had to take precautionary measures against in writing. Haco, King of Norway, granted the earldom of Orkney to the first Prince Henry, the son of Lord William by the daughter of the Earl of Ross. This Henry married first a daughter of the King of Denmark, without issue ; and next Jane Haliburton, daughter of Lord Haliburton, Dirleton Castle, Haddingtonshire, by whom he had Henry, Earl of Orkney. [This is the discoverer, but his father was William]. Henry married the fair Egidia, daughter of the famous Black Douglas by Egidia Stuart, daughter of King Robert the Second [by Elizabeth More the concubine]. Malise Grahame, second of the name, Earl of Stratherne, Orkney, and Caithness, was declared an outlaw and stripped of his titles and possessions by the Scottish king and parliament in 1344, for disposing of the earldom of Caithness to Earl Warenne, an Englishman, "the Scottish king's enemy," says Sir George Balfour, the Scotch genealogist and antiquary of the sixteenth century, as also say the state records. Caithness earldom thereafter remained crown property till Robert III. granted it to his half-brother Walter Stuart, Earl of Athole, as most jurists believe, the legitimate royal Stuart and proper king. Mackay gives 1420 as the date of Prince Henry the discoverer's death. He says the Sinclairs held the Orkneys under the Kings of Denmark ; and as they had also lands and titles in Scotland, these kings were jealous of them, and admitted their claims to the Orkneys under severe conditions and burdens. Of this severity the investitures show nothing really, though that interpretation might be taken by those unacquainted with feudalism. His other conclusion is sounder, namely, that the King of Scotland, because they were in homage to Denmark, and because of the exhorbitancy of their power, never would admit their claims to Caithness on the mainland of Scotland while they were the Princes of Orkney, but that they never dropped their rights to both. Such a claim strongly supports the growing impression that the discoverer's grandfather Prince Henry I. was also Earl of Caithness by courtesy, that is, by being the husband of the Countess of Caithness, a sole heiress, as the great antiquary Hearne has stated. Calder, p. 102, has a Norse theory of Sinclair Earls of Caithness from 1331. But on the claims and alliances of various families in the connection, see Dr Anderson's excellent discussions in his edition of the "Orkneyinga Saga," and, still better, see Bishop Tulloch of the fifteenth century himself in the "Bannatyne Miscellany." By help of the bishop's unprejudiced historical facts Sir Robert Gordon's "Short Discourse of the Earl of Sutherland's Precedence in Parliament before the Earls of Caithness," pp. 425-444 of his "Genealogy," written in 1630, can be also made most useful in exactly the contrary of its author's sinister intentions, so shaky a business is either deliberate lying or selfish enthusiasm. The facts of antiquity against which he fulminates he is the unconscious and outwitted instrument of recording ; which facts such writing as the bishop's thoroughly authenticates. In this vein Gordon's so-called "fabulous and forged reveries" turn out to be truths, and they can be read by his opposites to good purpose. The Earls of Caithness could trace back from Reginald, Earl of Möre (or Moray, "a plain"), in Norway, the father of Rollo, first Duke of Normandy, of whose male descent they were and are, coming from Normandy to England, to Scotland thence, and back again to Norseland. Even as a Seton, which Gordon was, he befooled himself; because the Setons were an English branch of the same stock as the house of Caithness; the Sutherland predecessors of the Gordons ancient, but *novi homines* to the Rollo lineage.

XI.

In Pinkerton's "History of Scotland," published at London in 1797, there is knowledge about Prince Henry the navigator and discoverer. He gives, from Torfaeus, the conditions of the investiture with the earldom of Orkney. The great-grandfather of Henry, Sir William, of Bannockburn fame, obtained the Orkneys, he wrongly thinks by marrying a daughter of the Earl of Stratherne, whose first name he makes Malise, though it was Julius, the Sparre favourite of the king. Prince Henry's death date he, also, gives as 1420. The next to him was William, "the celebrated Chancellor, who in 1470 surrendered the Orkneys to the Scottish crown. To this great man, who held the earldom when the cessation of it by Norway to Scotland was made, it may appear that Scotland was not a little indebted for this advantage." He says that the Kings of Denmark, who annexed Norway to their kingdom in 1387 (all Scandinavia, Sweden included, often under one king), were the superiors during most of the discoverer's time; and he gives the knowledge, already stated, that from 1422 to 1434 the Norse government appointed rulers over the Orkneys during the minority of Prince William, the Chancellor, 1434 his year of investiture by Eric, King of Denmark. It was Eric who ceded the Orkneys to James III. of Scotland, as marriage dowry with his daughter, Margaret. Pinkerton admits his obligations to Torfaeus for his facts, but he has used them to purpose. The light thrown on the discoverer's life by one passage of his obtains him credit for prescience, considering the time he wrote, at the end of last century, when there was no very strong interest connected with the question. Fiske has referred to him, but here is his meditation :—" In 1390 happened the strange voyage of Nicolo Zeno to Shetland ; [the book describing it] published at Venice, 1558, in octavo. The learned dissent much with regard to the veracity of the volume. If real, the author's

Frisland is the Faroe Islands, and his Zichmni is Sinclair. His book is one of the most puzzling in the whole circle of literature." The puzzle, thanks to Major, to Fiske, and to other Americans, has vanished, leaving a residuum of unmistakably important and permanent historical fact, a corner foundation stone of America's story, past and future. Among other narration, he says Bowar relates that Roslin Chapel was building when he wrote in 1444, and that Crawford officially dated the founding of it as 1441, Spottiswoode also agreeing; the service to be by a provost, six prebendaries, and two singing-boys.

Thomas Hearne [1678-1735], in his "Antiquities of Great Britain," says that Henry "succeeded to the honours and estates of his father, and, by marriage with the daughter and sole heiress of the Earl of Caithness, added the title of Prince of the Orkneys and of the lands of those islands, held at that time under the crown of Denmark, to his other dignities and possessions." This was the first Prince Henry, who, if Hearne is correct, was thus Earl of Caithness in right of his wife about 1322. Of the second, the discoverer of America, he says that he "succeeded to this principality, together with the barony of Roslin, and built the great dungeon or citadel at Roslin Castle, with many grand apartments. It is said the dignity of this prince was supported by an uncommonly great and splendid retinue, and that he was particularly munificent to the church. He gave lands to the abbey of Holyroodhouse sufficient for the maintenance of 7000 sheep, with a number of rich, embroidered cups, for the more honourable celebration of divine worship, and founded several churches besides within his barony. William, his son, after the death of this prince, lived in still greater splendour at Roslin." Hearne goes on with details about his generous pay to the builders he employed from all countries numerously, and mentions the date of the great fire which occurred at Roslin Castle, namely, 1447. But the narrative of the English antiquarian must not be followed beyond the discoverer, who, it may be added, gave gifts to Newbottle Abbey as well as to Holyrood Abbey.

The Harleian MS. 4238, has an account of the family of Sinclair, Earl of Orkney. In the Zeno book, Prince Henry is spoken of as also great in Scotland by title, as well as in the Scandinavian empire. He built a fort at Bressay Sound, where Cromwell afterwards erected one which is still existing, near where the chief town of Shetland is situated, Lerwick, then non-existent. Beatson's "Political Index" to the date of 1379 puts Sir Henry Sinclair, Earl of Orkney, and adds, "It seems uncertain whether this earldom reverted to the crown in 1471 by a surrender of the patent or a forfeiture. This 1379 creation was by Haco, King of Norway, but confirmed the same year by Robert II., King of Scotland." It has already been said that the marriage of James III. to Margaret of Denmark was the cause of annexation; and there is a quantity of documents in the state records of Scotland explaining the process of divesting William, who received Caithness earldom, Ravensheuch, and many other estates in Fifeshire and elsewhere as exchange for his principality.

When Alexander Ard, the son of Matilda Grahame, resigned Caithness and Strathearne earldoms and parts of Orkney to the crown, David Stuart, 2nd son of Robert II., had Caithness; and the third son Alexander by Elizabeth More the concubine, called "The Wolf of Badenoch" from his fierce character, was by charter of 1372 made king's lieutenant over all the north of Scotland to the Pentland Firth. Euphemia Ross, heiress of the earldom of Ross, brought the earldom of Scrathearne to Robert II., when she became Queen of Scotland as his wife; and it is through this Ross connection that the affairs of the Sinclairs intermingled so much with those of the royal Stuarts; the Ross rights to Caithness, &c., running to both families, as they did also to the Macdonald Lords of the Isles, with in this last case fatal results like the sanguinary battle of Harlaw, Aberdeenshire, in 1411.

XII.

"The Rolls of Scotland," carried to the Tower of London, and kept afterwards in the chapter-house of Westminster Abbey, but placed now in the Record Office, Fetter Lane, London, have many notices of the discoverer. King Richard II. of England gave a safe-conduct or passport to Henry, Earl of Orkney and Lord of Roslin, from 10th March, 1391-2, to Michaelmas, with permission to be accompanied by 24 persons, the necessary horses, &c., with proviso that no one fleeing the English laws should be of the company. The king signed it at Leeds Castle, Kent. January 30th, 1405-6, Henry IV. signed a safe-conduct for 13 Scottish magnates, among whom was Henry, Earl of Orkney, 50 persons allowed as their company. The magnates were to be hostages for the Earl of Douglas, who was to go to Scotland. He had been taken prisoner by the English king in aiding Percy's rebellion, and was ultimately freed by ransom. John Stuart, son of the Regent of Scotland (the Duke of Albany), and Sir William Sinclair, the latter the son of Prince Henry by Florentia of Denmark, were two of those hostages. On 15th March, 1406, the same king, from Westminster, gave a safe-conduct to Henry, Earl of Orkney, and to Walter, Lord Haliburton, to come into England with 40 persons, to stay till the feast of St. John the Baptist. Of date Westminster, 8th April, 1407, Henry IV. signed passport to Patrick Thomson and Henry Shipman, the masters of a ship from Scotland, and to Alexander Johnson and Robert Black, of Scotland, with 12 persons accompanying them to London by ship with goods and merchandise coming with Henry, Earl of Orkney. On the supplication of Henry, Earl of Orkney, Alexander Ledale, and Robert Williamson, armorials-bearing gentlemen and followers of that earl, had a safe-conduct with 8 persons by sea and land within England, dated by private seal at Westminster, 4th January, 1407-8, from Henry the Usurper or IV., the permission to last till Pentecost. Of date 14th April, 1416, Henry V., at Westminster, London, gave his protection in England till 15th August to Henry, Earl of Orkney, with 20 persons, coming from and returning to Scotland.

When Henry V. was going to France in 1421, he gave permission to James I. of Scotland, England's prisoner then 15 years, to visit his country, of date Westminster, 31st May, for three months, with hostages 20 in number in his room, 5 of them earls; William, Earl of Orkney, one of these. This favour was at the instigation of the Earl of Douglas. The special point to notice in reference to the biography of the discoverer here, is that he died before 31st May, 1421, instead of in 1422, as Fordun says; for his son William, by this record of state, was then described as Earl of Orkney. King James was not finally freed to go to his kingdom until 1423, after 17 years of detention from his capture by Henry IV. in 1406.

It is not known, however, that he thus visited his country at intervals on the hostage principle; and Henry's frequent visits to England, must have been in his capacity of hereditary tutor to the Princes of Scotland.

Henry's brother John had a safe-conduct from Henry V. to come to England with 12 persons of any rank, to treat about the King of Scotland's return and his own going to France in 1421. On 15th May, 1412, from Westminster, Henry V. had given him a passport for himself and two others, the party to be 20 persons while in England. Again and again Sir John appears as one of Scotland's wise men, brother of the discoverer of America, both of them well known in European courts as accomplished chiefs of their time. From Windsor Richard II. gave a safe-conduct to Sir John, this brother, as ambassador, and to three others, with 60 horses, on 24th July, 1392, "to discuss negotiations with our Scotch enemies." Henry IV. from Pontefract, Yorkshire, on 30th June, 1404, gave Sir John a passport for a quarter of a year; and again, from Leicester, 2nd August, 1404, till Easter. From Tutbury one is granted to him and two others, 13th September, 1404, till paschal feast, with twelve persons. Richard II. from Westminster, 23rd October, 1395, gave him passport for a year, with 13 followers on horseback. He, Lord Dundas, Robert Trofort, and 12 servants, with the Earl of Douglas, had passport from Henry IV. dated Westminster, 28th September, 1406, which must have been for getting James I. of Scotland out of Henry IV. the King of England's hands, after his inhospitable, perfidious capture a few months before, together with his guardian, the Admiral of Scotland, Prince Henry of Orkney. Sir John and others, with 12 persons, had a safe-conduct on 16th July, 1413, when Henry V. had just come to the throne (hope long given up of the clemency of his father, the Lancastrian Henry IV.), to negotiate "for the delivery of the King of Scotland." They were on their way to France. At Westminster Henry V. on 19th August, 1413, gave permission to Sir John to carry through England to Scotland a quantity of *armaturas*, that is, coats of mail and fighting accoutrements. These brothers were as familiar in Southern as they were in Northern Europe, France being a happy hunting-ground for the Scotch in particular. Sir John with William Cockburn had another passport of date 20th July, 1413, to last till the following Easter,

x

with 12 followers.   On 9th June, 1421, at Dover, Henry the Fifth gave him 30 lancers, and a safe-conduct, going to Rouen in Normandy with himself and King James I. of Scotland.   Sir John's brother Prince Henry was then dead, as has been seen ; and the "Rolls of Scotland" are entirely silent about Sir John also after this entry.   He seems to have exerted himself greatly for the cultivated poet-king, though without effect up to the 1421 date.

Capper, in his "Topographical Dictionary," published at London in 1808, says the chapel of Roslin Castle "was founded in 1446 by the Prince of Orkney and Duke of Oldenburg."   This was William, the first Earl of Caithness, by the ordinary reckoning.   Of the castle it is said that it was "the favourite of the great family."   The "Edinburgh Gazetteer" of 1822 gives the dimensions of the chapel as 69 feet long, 34 broad, and 40 high ; its marvellous internal beauty quite taking away the realisation of its smallness, by admiration for its harmony.

XIII.

In conclusion, it may be asked what modern or Caithnessian value has these gatherings of antiquarianism.   The brief account in the first chapter might have been enough.   But to some of the brightest minds of America the burning question has of late been whether the Latin or Saxon race is to have the supremacy of their country ; the intense activity of Roman Catholicism contrasted with the apathy of Protestantism giving philosophers and statesmen pause as to the near results, notwithstanding the power of science and reason.   The glorification of Columbus in the discovery centenary of 1892 was an aid towards the threatened Spanish or Latin domination ; and Scandinavian energy has been in movement, especially at the Chicago Exhibition of 1893, to counteract the southern tide, by ascribing the discovery of America to Norsemen of the Teuton stock, including, as principal factors, the English and the Dutch. Caithnessmen, especially of Canada and the United States, have the strongest personal interest in such a gigantic Armageddon contest of blood and belief, if it is to be early fact.   That the ancestor of many of them, and one in affinity with more, such as Mowats, Bremners (*e.g.*, the naval officer mentioned in the preface, now of the Centurion, flagship, China, who was kinship to Hon. Robert Sinclair, Wick), Cormacks, Millers, Sutherlands, Bruces, Keiths, and others, is the principal figure to oppose to the renowned Italian Christopher, makes Prince Henry Sinclair II. of as much present as past relation, not only to district, but to the widest of the world's movements; parochialism not the note of the northern vikings, roving now for property, knowledge, and rule as of yore.

EXPLANATION.

WHEN "Caithness Events" had been quite finished for press, a revelation came from the noteworthy acumen of Bailie Charles Bruce, F.S.A., Scot. He had remembered reading the Kennedy MS. in print more than fifty years ago, and after putting his brain on the rack as to where, discovered that it had appeared in the *John O'Groat Journal* on the following dates, namely, 2nd February, 2nd March, 1st May, 2nd June, 3rd August, 16th September, 14th October, 1836 ; 31st March, 2nd June, 20th October, 1837 ; and 16th February, 20th April, 7th, 14th, 21st September, 2nd, 16th November, 1838. If this takes away the prestige of first publication, the long period since the MS. was printed, and the inaccessibility of it to the public, in the practically buried old columns of a newspaper, are ample reasons for its reappearance. It is an ordinary thing, besides, for journalistic contributions to be republished in book form to insure permanence for good material. The same kindly authority has further favoured with the following :—"The editor of the *John O'Groat Journal* at the time was Benjamin Miller Kennedy, a son of Captain Kennedy, the compiler of the MS. Captain Kennedy had two sons and three daughters. One of the sons died in Berbice, British Guiana. Benjamin left Wick, established the *Guide* newspaper, Arbroath, and died there. Neither of the brothers was married. Of the daughters, Isabella married Captain Macpherson, the Lieutenant A. Macpherson of the Caithness Legion. See Calder's ' History of Caithness.' He died in 1869, aged 100. Louisa married William Davidson, fishcurer, Wick. He died in 1832. Mrs Davidson and family soon after went to America. Marion married William Waters, many years bailie and afterwards for a short time, from February, 1858, provost of Wick. He and his wife resided in the house built for Captain Kennedy by the grandfather of Mrs. Waters, James Taylor, master-builder of the town about the end of last century. Her brother Benjamin lived with them, and kept up regular correspondence after he went to Arbroath." Additional knowledge exists in letters between Provost Waters and Donald Horne of Langwell about shares which Captain Kennedy held in the British Fisheries Society. As they were written in consequence of his death, and the title of captain is expressly used in them, it is clear that the attachment of major to his name on the back of the MS., by another and later hand than his, was a mistake. A letter by the son Benjamin, in which there is a paragraph relating to the MS., and copies both of the will of 1833 and settlement of estate in 1835 of the son Robert, still survive, as well as tacks and other documents, in which " Captain " Kennedy is mentioned.

THE END.

WORKS BY THE SAME AUTHOR.

Poems. Crown 8vo., cloth, 5s.

"Possess very high merit. They are the outcome not only of deep feeling, but of feeling in such inner harmony with the beautiful and the good, that they can bring the reader into the same fellowship."—*Leeds Mercury.*

LONDON : PROVOST & Co.

The Messenger. Foolscap 8vo., cloth, 5s.

"Rich in poetic feeling, and still richer in its future promise."—*Newcastle Chronicle.*

Love's Trilogy. Crown 8vo., cloth 5s.

"A solid piece of the best workmanship."—*Brighton Gazette.*

The Mount. Crown 8vo., cloth 10s.

"Evidently holds the real secret of Shakespeare's worth.—*Glasgow Herald.*

Goddess Fortune. Three vols. Post 8vo., cloth, 31s 6d.

"It is rarely that so much philosophical treatise is given to the world in the shape of a novel. . . insight that is very reflective, keen, and sure."—*Morning Advertiser.*

Quest. Crown, 8vo., cloth, 2s 6d.

"Varied as the subjects are, the writer touches them with a light and delicate hand ; his thought is suggestive ; and the book bristles with sentences and passages which the reader instinctively stops to question, to wonder at, or to admire."—*Dundee Advertiser.*

Humanities. Crown 8vo., cloth, 3s 6d.

"Those who do not agree with the author's views will find much to appreciate in his literary studies and his impressions of travel."—*Westminster Review.*

Essays in Three Kinds. Crown 8vo., cloth, 1s 6d.

"The writer's ability is manifest."—*Athenæum.*

LONDON : TRUBNER & Co.

Humanitatstudien. Crown 8vo., 2s 6d.

"To the German translation of 'Humanities,' which, so far as we have examined it, seems to be well done, Herr Müller has prefixed a graceful preface, in which he gives a brief account of the author, and his own reasons for translating the work."—*Scottish Review.*

STRASBURG : KARL J. TRUBNER.

Travel Sketch. Crown 8vo., 6s.

"Exceptionally interesting, because it combines all the vivid, vigorous realism of the impressionist school of work with a philosophical reflectiveness and acute perception which make the word pictures reveal the very spirit and character of the places and persons concerned."—*Vanity Fair.*

LONDON : KEGAN PAUL & Co.

The Sinclairs of England. Crown 8vo., cloth, 12s.

"A volume full of recondite learning, and written withal in a free and popular style of narrative not often exemplified in such works."—*Scotsman.*

LONDON : QUARITCH.

The Gunns. Foolscap 4to., cloth, 5s.

"A very valuable contribution to the historical records of the north."—*People's Journal.*

WICK : RAE.

WORKS PRINTED AND PUBLISHED BY W. RAE.

Ministers and Men In the Far North. By Rev. ALEX. AULD, F.C. Minister of Olrig. Crown 8vo. (sold out).

Second Edition of ditto. Edinburgh : JOHN MENZIES & Co., 3s.

Memorials of David Steven. By Rev. ALEX. AULD, F.C. Minister of Olrig. Foolscap 8vo., 1s.

"I have read every word of the 'Memoir of David Stephen' with great interest. He has been an extraordinary man. We have not many like him in England. In travelling in Scotland I always meet with shrewd intelligent men of his class."—JOHN BRIGHT, M.P.

History of Caithness. By JAMES T. CALDER. Crown 8vo., 5s 6d.

"This is a book of great historical and traditionary interest and of considerable literary merit. . . . . It is somewhat surprising that for more than twenty years a work of so much real value and so full of interest to natives of Caithness especially has been allowed to lie in dark oblivion. At last, however, thanks to the enterprise of the present publisher, Mr. Rae of Wick, this new edition has appeared, got up in good form and with its attractions and usefulness enhanced by a map and illustrations and by the addition of many useful notes by Mr. Thomas Sinclair. . . . . The book contains many fine legends, with a charming strain of romance in them "—*Scotsman.*

Salvation Applied. By Rev. GEORGE STEVENSON, F.C. Minister of Pulteneytown, 1s.

Contemporary Socialism. By JOHN RAE, M.A. Crown 8vo., 10s 6d.

"Mr Rae's 'Contemporary Socialism' has justly earned the repute of being the most thorough exposition of modern socialistic thought and action which is to be found in the English language. . . . . The good qualities of the former edition are preserved. The fairness with which the various authors criticised have their opinions stated, and the thoroughness with which their views are examined and tested ; and to these qualities the work of revision has brought additional care of statement and fullness of exposition."—*Journal of the Royal Statistical Society.*

Memorabilia Domestica ; or Parish Life in the North of Scotland. By Rev. ALEX. SAGE, Minister of Resolis. Demy 8vo., 7s 6d. (A few copies only left.)

The Rev. Dr. Aird, ex-Moderator of the Free Church, referring to this work, writes the publisher as follows :—"I was enchanted with it. I intimated on Sabbath last in Gaelic to my own congregation that it had appeared, and exhorted all who could to get a copy of it. Your part has been executed particularly well, the paper and type are very good, and also the cloth binding quite substantial and neat. The Sutherland, Caithness, and Ross people ought to buy the first edition in six weeks time. I am sure a thousand copies would be sold in a short time in Canada, where there are so many of the descendants of evicted persons from the above counties. I am sure that the minute description of the topography of Kildonan in chapter VI. will be very interesting to the descendants of those who at one time inhabited it."

The Bible : A Lecture for Young Men. By Rev. GEORGE RENNY, F.C. Minister, Wick, 3d.

Poems. By G. W. LEVACK. Foolscap 8vo., 1s.

The Gunns. By Thomas Sinclair, M.A. Foolscap 4to., 5s.

"In this handsome volume of 211 quarto pages, Mr Sinclair presents, not a history of the Gunn clan, but rather the raw material of that history. He collects the fragmentary reference to the Gunns which have appeared in other works, extracts from public documents and private papers, and a considerable quantity of traditional lore, and critically compares and examines them ; and he traces the various branches of the family at home and in Ireland. The Gunns took part in all the feuds of the Mackays and Sutherlands and Sinclairs, and other northern clans and landed families, and thus their history becomes practically the history of the north of Scotland, and to that Mr Sinclair's volume is an important contribution."—*Orkney Herald.*

Wick : In and Around It. By Rev. John Horne. 6d.

"A handsomely printed little Note-book, distinctly outside the ordinary guide-book rut in style," and one that "the visitor will peruse with interest and pleasure."—*Northern Chronicle.*

The Diversions of an Autograph-Hunter. By J. H., Wick, 2s.

"This is an amusing little book. The author seems to have had a wide experience as an autograph-hunter, and he writes of his hobby with enthusiasm and humour."—*Glasgow Herald.*

The Kennedy M.S. Discussed, with an Account of the Broynach Earls, etc. By Thomas Sinclair, M.A. Foolscap 4to., 5s.